Liz Lange's Maternity Style

HOW TO LOOK FABULOUS DURING THE MOST FASHION-CHALLENGED TIME

Liz Lange

Clarkson Potter/Publishers
New York

I DEDICATE THIS BOOK TO MY TWO BEAUTIFUL CHILDREN, GUS AND ALICE, TRULY THE BEST PART OF BEING PREGNANT. AND TO MY HUSBAND, JEFF, WITHOUT WHOM GUS AND ALICE AND ALL OF THIS WOULD NOT BE POSSIBLE.

Published by Clarkson Potter/Publishers, New York, New York.
Member of the Crown Publishing Group, a division of Random House, Inc.
www.randomhouse.com

CLARKSON N. POTTER is a trademark and POTTER and colophon
are registered trademarks of Random House, Inc.

Printed in Singapore

Design by Jane Wagman/Janedesign, Inc.
Text by Jenifer Berman
Illustrations by Stephen Campbell for Art Department
Still life photographs by Coppola + Grande

Library of Congress Cataloging-in-Publication Data
Available upon request.

ISBN 0-609-80917-2

10 9 8 7 6 5 4 3 2 1

First Edition

acknowledgments

There are a number of people who helped me in the development of this book and who contributed to its exciting completion. For her ongoing support I thank Pam Bernstein, my agent, who first suggested this book (a long time ago!); Margot Schupf, the editor who first believed in the book and helped shape it; and Katie Workman, my editor at Clarkson Potter, who always knows what works and what doesn't and who shepherded this book to completion.

There are so many people without whom this book would not be possible: Jane Wagman, my amazing and fabulously tasteful art director; Jenifer Berman, who always knew just the right thing to say; Sandra Hamburg, who found such beautiful images; and Dorit Morley, my stylist extraordinaire. I don't know what I would have done without all of you.

I am so grateful to all of the women who generously supplied quotes for this book and who shared so much about this personal time in their lives with me. You've been so supportive from the very beginning, and it has been such a pleasure to know all of you and to work with so many of you during your pregnancies.

I could never have found the time to work on this project if it hadn't been for the help and support of the staff at Liz Lange Maternity. Everyone there has been unbelievable: Becky Bauer, Jessica Gold, Barbara Lerman, Natalie Markoff, and the whole gang.

Major thanks to the following individuals and organizations, not just for their help with this book but for all of their continued help and support over the last five years: my parents, Kathy and Bob Steinberg; my sister Jane; Kathie Bannon; Jeff Cohen; Barry Ginsburg; Janet Crown Peterson; the wonderful women's apparel team at Nike, in particular Mindy Grossman, Heidi O'Neill, and Jamie Shierk; all of my great friends at Target (too many of you to mention by name); Jacquie Tractenberg, my close friend and my publicist; Michael Solomon; Betsy Radin; Melissa Krinzman; Jonathan Adler; Simon Doonan; and my wonderfully supportive husband, Jeff Lange.

A huge thank you to all of the magazine and newspaper editors who have shown such unflagging support since the very beginning.

I'd also like to recognize all the maternity brands (aside from my own) whose clothes we used in creating this book: Annacris, Babystyle, Barney's Procreation, Belly Basics, Chaiken, Duo from JC Penney, Emma & Me, First Comes Love, Gap, Japanese Weekend, L'Attesa, Limor & Juliet, Majamas, Mimi Maternity, Mommy Chic, Motherhood Maternity, Mother Two Be, Old Navy, A Pea in the Pod, Pumpkin Maternity, Target, and Veronique.

Finally, kudos to all who celebrate and support pregnant women and who share my enthusiasm for this momentous time.

contents

preface

Pregnancy style. To some this idea seems baffling, but to me it's always made perfect sense. Pregnant women are beautiful, and pregnancy is undoubtedly one of the happiest, sexiest, and most exciting times in a woman's life. In my mind, a pregnant woman should be celebrated, in every way, so I've never understood why maternity clothes needed to be so incredibly unattractive. Remember those ruffles and bows? I do, and it's the reason I began designing my own maternity wear line. It's also the reason I've written this book.

There's absolutely no reason a woman must sacrifice her sense of style just because she's pregnant. She shouldn't have to dress like a child just because she's having a child; it's one thing to put a toddler in a sailor suit, but it's another thing completely to condemn a grown woman to such a fate. Instead, a woman should be able to dress as she would in her normal life, wearing chic, simple American clothes. More importantly, those clothes should show off—rather than hide—an expecting woman's body. Not only do more fitted clothes make you look thinner (a definite plus!), but they also assert that pregnancy is a natural, beautiful, and sensual state.

So how to use this book? Most important is knowing that achieving the Liz Lange look is a philosophy and not a price tag. You don't have to spend a thousand dollars on maternity wear to look great when you're pregnant, and any woman can achieve a fabulous sense of style no matter how large or small her budget. Together, we can create a wardrobe that focuses on ease, elegance, economy, and comfort; a wardrobe that's built around a few good pieces that can take you through any number of occasions: work, weekends, evening, travel, holidays, and special occasions.

When I was pregnant, both with my son and daughter, I learned how important it was to simplify my life—and especially my wardrobe. There's nothing worse than opening a jam-packed closet to find nothing to wear, so I hope this book helps you find a few great looks that you can turn to again and again. I also hope it helps to debunk a few old myths: a pregnant woman doesn't need to hide behind oversized clothes; she doesn't need to dress like a little girl; she doesn't need to have a new outfit for every occasion; she doesn't need to spend a lot of money to look good.

When you're pregnant, everyone always talks about the miracle of life and how being a mother is the most important job you'll ever have. And while that's true, no one ever speaks frankly about what you're going to wear. Since I started my line in 1997, it's been such a pleasure working with women and helping them find creative ways to feel stylish and "normal" during their pregnancies. Thanks to all who have let me share in their excitement, and congratulations to all the moms-to-be.

Liz Lange

how to use the book: a key

It's easy! The book is divided into chapters that focus on the active parts of your life, proving that pregnancy style can be everyday style. In each chapter, there are a number of recurring essentials that will help show you the way.

Maternity Must Have
An item no pregnant woman should be without. The backbone of your wardrobe.

Quotes
Celebrities weigh in on their pregnancy experiences and style survival tactics.

Mix and Match
The cardinal rule of pregnancy. Ideas on how to exponentially increase the number of outfits in your wardrobe.

Trimester Mini-Chapters
One stage at a time, a trip down the winding road of pregnancy, from the moment you pee on the stick to the moment you fit back into your favorite pair of jeans.

Question and Answer
My responses to frequently asked questions from clients from around the country.

Save vs. Splurge
When to bargain shop and when to treat yourself. Advice on how to look like a knockout without batting your budget out of the park.

Accessories: Wardrobe enhancers that turn humdrum into hey-now.

a brief timeline of maternity fashion

Ancient Egypt
MATERNITY CLOTHES?
WHAT MATERNITY CLOTHES?
WOMEN LET IT ALL HANG OUT.

Roman Empire
TOGAS ARE ALL THE RAGE.
PERFECT FOR DISGUISING
A BULGING BELLY.

Renaissance
MAMMA MIA. HIGH-WAISTED STYLES
ARE IN VOGUE ALL OVER EUROPE.
EASY ATTIRE FOR EXPECTING WOMEN.

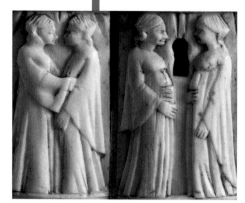

Classic Greece
CHILTONS ARE CHIC. OVERSIZED TUNICS
ARE TERRIFIC FOR EXPECTING MOTHERS.

Middle Ages
RELIGIOUS ICONOGRAPHY
ABOUNDS. DEPICTIONS
OF PREGNANT WOMEN
RESEMBLE THE MADONNA.

Eighteenth Century
HERE COMES THE CORSET. MARIE ANTOINETTE AND HER DISCIPLES HELD IT IN WITH PANNIERS AND STAYS. CAN YOU IMAGINE?

Victorian Era
THE CORSET RETURNS WITH A VENGEANCE. MODESTY RULES THE DAY AND MATERNITY FASHION FALLS PREY TO THE WASP-WAIST.

Turn of the Century
IN WITH THE BELLE EPOQUE. ART NOUVEAU AND ORIENTAL TUNICS WORK WONDERS FOR EXPECTING WOMEN.

French Revolution
ALL HAIL THE EMPIRE. EMPRESS JOSEPHINE USHERS IN (FINALLY!) A LOOSE, FREE-FLOWING LOOK.

American Frontier
WESTWARD HO! PIONEER WOMEN—EVEN MARY INGALLS— ASSERT THEIR INDEPENDENCE WITH ROOMY TRAIL DRESSES PERFECT FOR PREGNANCY.

Roaring Twenties
FLAPPER FASHIONS.
THE GARÇONNE STYLE
TAKES HOLD WITH
MATERNITY-FRIENDLY
LONG-WAISTED LOOKS.

Forties
RAYON ARRIVES AND SHIRTDRESSES ARE IN.
NEW SYNTHETIC FABRICS THAT STRETCH
MAKE MATERNITY CLOTHES AN EASY FIT.

Thirties
THE FIRST REAL
MATERNITY
CLOTHES!
AMERICAN
DEPARTMENT
STORES INTRO-
DUCE A NEW
CATEGORY IN
WOMEN'S WEAR.

"SHE'S GOING TO HAVE A BABY"

Fifties
BABY ON BOARD.
POST-WAR AMERICAN
MOTHERS-TO-BE
FAVOR INNOCENT
LOOKS SUCH AS
COLLARS AND BOWS.
SCHIAPARELLI SAVES
THE DAY WITH TUNIC
DRESSES AND FULL-
CUT JACKETS OVER
LONG, SLIM SKIRTS.

Sixties
HIGH TIMES FOR MATERNITY WEAR.
YVES SAINT LAURENT INTRODUCES THE
TRAPEZIUM SHAPE. BRIGHT COLORS,
SHORTER SKIRTS, AND CAPRIS TAKE COMMAND.

Eighties
FASHION DISASTER! SHOULDER
PADS VIE WITH PINAFORE DRESSES
IN PREGNANT WOMEN'S CLOSETS.
WHAT MORE CAN YOU SAY?

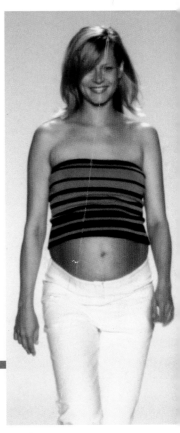

Seventies
FLOWER POWER.
HIPPIE FASHION
TAKES HOLD WITH
FREE-FLOWING
SKIRTS, SMOCKS,
AND YOKE DRESSES
THAT EASILY
ACCOMMODATE A
GROWING BELLY.

Today
CELEBRATE! YOU'VE
ARRIVED! A VIEW
FROM THE FIRST
MATERNITY RUNWAY
SHOW IN NEW YORK.

Nineties
A NEW ERA. STYLE AND MATERNITY
ARE FINALLY IN SYNC WITH HIP,
BODY-CONSCIOUS FASHIONS THAT
LET YOU BE WHO YOU WANT TO BE.

13   LIZ LANGE'S MATERNITY STYLE

work

Women work. Today it's no longer the anomaly; it's the norm. Working women—working *pregnant* women—are a common sight in the office, and apart from the occasional afternoon nap, many women work right up until their water breaks. If you fall into this bring-home-the-bacon category, you may need to elevate your feet from time to time, but everyone agrees, your doctor or midwife included, working is a great way to keep your mind active and distracted from various pregnancy anxieties.

The question for professional women, then, is how to look like a corporate tiger when you're really feeling like an overstuffed kangaroo? The answer is to go clean and finished. That's the watchword for the workplace. Women have come way too far to hide behind large and unfashionable clothes for nine months. Today we are lawyers, doctors, editors, professors, and corporate executives. We command authority and respect, and the clothes we wear need to reflect that.

Work clothes, therefore, may be the one area where you will want to spend a little money. To look polished and professional can require some selective purchasing. You by all means don't need to go on a spending spree, but when you're standing in front of a boardroom filled with pinstripe-suited men, I guarantee you'll be happy that you spent a little extra on the right jacket and coordinating skirt.

"WHEN IN DOUBT: BLACK, BLACK, AND MORE BLACK."
– LARA SPENCER, *GOOD MORNING AMERICA*

find your uniform

Every pregnant working woman knows that you need to find the one look that works for you. This is your foundation, the outfit you can turn to with ease on those mornings when the idea of getting out of bed seems like an Everest-sized effort. One of my customers who works as a magazine editor relied on a pair of black pants, a tailored man's-style shirt, and a merino-blend cardigan. With shirts in a couple of pretty colors, she always had a combination that worked.

The important thing to remember is that no one expects you to have a new outfit every day when you're pregnant. The concepts of rotating and recycling go a long way. Everyone knows that maternity clothes are a short-term investment, and even in the most conservative of offices, the same one or two suits will be just fine as long as they're clean and in good shape.

suit up

If you do work in a conservative environment, a suit is probably required. This may seem daunting—both physically and fiscally—but the good news is that today's maternity suits are simpler, more professional looking, and designed to complement your growing figure. Just start with the essentials. Buy the dress, the skirt and/or the pants, and the jacket. You now have several variations on a basic foundation, and with a few simple sweaters and a couple of pretty blouses, you have more than a week's worth of office attire. Also, in the early or even mid-months of your pregnancy, feel free to use your regular blazers—just wear them open.

"MY MUST-HAVE ITEM DURING PREGNANCY WAS A PAIR OF BEAUTIFUL BUT COMFORTABLE SLIM PANTS. I COULD DRESS THEM UP WITH HEELS OR DOWN WITH FLATS."
— DEBORAH ROBERTS, *20/20*

Underpinnings such as blouses, shirts, and sweaters should be nice and fitted. Make sure the shoulders match yours correctly. This is not the time or place to be wearing your husband's oxford.

The suit jacket is the most important component and will be noticed far more than a pair of pants. Look for set-in sleeves and traditional, soft tailoring. A strong-shouldered "power" look is particularly unflattering on a pregnant woman.

Tall black boots are a favorite of mine. When matched with a knee-length skirt, they lend a modern twist to conservative attire.

Simple shells and sweaters go perfectly under suits. Look for crewnecks, V-necks, and turtlenecks. Just keep the cleavage to a minimum—save that for after work!

If your budget allows, you can also build on your basics with a longer dress coat. Paired with a skirt or a dress of the same length, it's a feminine yet professional look.

Slim skirts work best. If your office allows, I tend to like a shorter hemline. Something around knee length, or just above the knee, if you can, looks great when you're pregnant.

Cardigans and twin sets are also excellent options. They are always appropriate, never severe, and you'll wear them again and again both at work and on the weekends. Go for neutral colors and a fairly fitted shape.

You can't go wrong with a simple single-breasted suit jacket. Not only is the look long and lean (aka slimming), but it does wonders at reducing wider hips and a fuller bust.

If you're going to buy one suit, buy it in charcoal gray. This classic tone is ultimately versatile and much softer (and less lint attracting) than black.

Suit pants should be skinny. A good cigarette pant with a slight flare or a boot cut is my personal choice. Stay away from oversized palazzo pants. They just look sloppy.

"I WAS DEFINITELY SHOWING BY TWO MONTHS! I WORK IN A PRETTY CASUAL ENVIRONMENT AND WORE LOTS OF FLOATY, FEMININE SKIRTS WITH LOW WAISTS AND SOMEWHAT FITTED BUT NOT TINY TEES. I THINK YOU HAVE TO GET INTO HAVING A SEXY LITTLE STOMACH AND SHOWING IT OFF; OTHERWISE YOU'RE STUCK LOOKING UNCOMFORTABLY HUGE."

— JEAN GODFREY-JUNE, BEAUTY EDITOR, *LUCKY*

SHAKING HANDS
AND MAKING
BABIES: QUEEN
RAINA OF JORDAN.

"TODAY'S CHICISSIMO MATERNITY CLOTHES PROVIDE THE PERFECT WORKING UNIFORMS FOR FASHION VICTIMS LIKE MYSELF: BLACK STRETCH PANTS, CASHMERE CARDIGAN SWEATER, AND A COTTON BUTTON-DOWN SHIRT."

– KATE BETTS, FASHION WRITER

Stockings

I've never met a pair of maternity stockings I liked. I know that in some office environ-ments stockings are required, even in the summer, but my advice is to stay away from the maternity brands. My clients have a much better time buying their favorite brand in an extra-large size. L'eggs queen-size, I've heard, are particularly good. Thigh highs are another great and comfortable option if the idea of constricting your belly is just too much.

"MY PREGNANCIES PREDATED THE
MINUTES, UNFORTUNATELY. I COULDN'T
STORES WITH CUTE PUNS IN THEIR
JUST WHAT A PREGNANT WOMAN
AND INSTEAD I IMPROVISED. IN THE
WAISTBANDS WITH RUBBER BANDS
AROUND HOOKS. LARGE SAFETY PINS
PREGNANCY PROGRESSED, I ENDED UP
I LIVED IN A BLACK CASHMERE
A WRAP SKIRT AND JACKET, AND A
A BROCADE COAT FOR COCKTAIL
CLOTHES MADE ME LOOK A BIT TOO
YEARS—BIG AND SQUARE IN THE BODY
BUT I DID WHAT I COULD."

DESIGNER MATERNITY TREND BY A FEW
BEAR THOSE MATERNITY CLOTHES FROM
NAMES (MY FAVORITE ONE WAS BALLOON—
DOESN'T WANT TO BE COMPARED TO!),
FIRST FOUR MONTHS, I JURY-RIGGED MY
LOOPED THROUGH BUTTONHOLES AND
WERE ALSO ESSENTIAL. AS EACH
BUYING CLOTHES A SIZE OR TWO LARGER.
TURTLENECK AND AN ELASTIC-WAIST SKIRT,
BLACK TRAPEZE DRESS TOPPED WITH
PARTIES. I'M SURE SOME OF THESE
MUCH LIKE MARLON BRANDO IN HIS LATER
WITH LITTLE LEGS STICKING OUT BELOW—
— LINDA WELLS, EDITOR-IN-CHIEF,
ALLURE

1

A TUNIC IS AN EXCEL-LENT ALTERNATIVE TO THE SUIT JACKET.

2

THE BLACK JACKET MAKES ANY OUTFIT MEAN BUSINESS.

3

A STREAMLINED KNIT DRESS IN BASIC CHARCOAL GRAY.

4

THE TRADITIONAL PENCIL SKIRT IS NEAT AND PROFESSIONAL.

5

BLACK CIGARETTE PANTS GO WITH EVERYTHING.

**1 + 4 =
at your desk**

**1 + 5 =
staff meeting**

**2 + 5 =
the pitch**

nine to five

I read once that Anna Wintour, the editor-in-chief of *Vogue,* buys a few outfits at the beginning of each season and simply wears them again and again. This is a good lesson, especially for a pregnant woman. If the leading lady of the fashion world can depend on a few key pieces to take her through her busy schedule, then so can you. You have to remember that although work sometimes seems to command your life, it's only five days you have to dress for. The intervening weekend does wonders at cleaning a fashion slate, so even if you have only a select number of pieces in your wardrobe, you should be able to come up with a number of suitable outfits that can take you through the week.

**2 + 4 =
client lunch**

**3 =
fall favorite**

**2 + 3 =
boardroom
presentation**

"ON THE SET I NEEDED BRIGHT COLORS THAT WOULD STAND OUT FOR THE CAMERAS. THERE'S ALSO THAT EXTRA FIVE (TO TEN!) POUNDS THE CAMERA GIVES YOU, SO I NEEDED TO BE VERY CAREFUL ABOUT KEEPING IT SLIM. TIGHTER-FITTING CLOTHES MADE ME LOOK THINNER, I THINK, OR AT LEAST MADE ME FEEL GOOD ABOUT MYSELF."

– KELLY RIPA,
LIVE WITH REGIS AND KELLY

On the Job
TOP ROW: KELLY RIPA ON THE SET OF *LIVE WITH REGIS AND KELLY*; POLITICAL CONSULTANT KARENNA GORE SCHIFF; TALK SHOW HOST RICKI LAKE. BOTTOM ROW: TELEVISION PERSONALITY KATHIE LEE GIFFORD; QUEEN RAINA OF JORDAN; ACTRESS/AUTHOR ANNE HECHE

the no-fail outfit

You've been preparing all month for an important pitch. The presentations are ready. Clients are flying in from all over the country, and it's up to you to seal the deal. If this isn't an occasion for a little splurge, I don't know what is. There are moments in every working woman's life when she needs to add a little pizzazz and personality to her everyday attire. For your moments in the spotlight, make sure you have a great outfit that makes you feel chic and in control.

DON'T UNDERESTIMATE THE IMPACT OF CASHMERE.
A GORGEOUS WRAP IN WINTER WHITE ADDS A KNOWING AIR TO
AN EVERYDAY SWEATER OR A STANDBY LITTLE BLACK DRESS.

LEATHER SAYS SOPHISTICATION. IT SAYS CONFIDENCE. IT SAYS
"LISTEN TO ME." ALTHOUGH NOT APPROPRIATE FOR ALL OFFICES,
IN A MORE LIBERAL ENVIRONMENT IT SPEAKS VOLUMES WHEN
PAIRED WITH AN UNDERSTATED TOP.

accessories

**Stack heels.
Pearls.
A red leather bag.
Choose items that
help you look pulled together.
A small pump.
Simple hoops.
Punch up an outfit
with a scarf, or
tie a cardigan around your
shoulders for a little
burst of color.**

color coded

Unless your job requires you to stand out in a crowd, I suggest you adopt a more neutral palette for your office attire. Gray, charcoal, navy, chocolate, olive, camel, and even a clever red can be excellent choices, especially when combined in a monochromatic way. By selecting understated pieces in similar tones, and mixing and matching fabrics, you can easily achieve a business-like look.

Q+A

Question: I just found out I'm pregnant. I'm thrilled, but want to keep it under wraps at the office until I'm at least through the first trimester. If I could still wear my old clothes it would be much easier, but already it seems I can't fit into anything. What to do?
— Cecilia, Denver, CO

Answer: Don't panic. Your first trimester is definitely a no-woman's-land, neither here nor there when it comes to size, but disguising your pregnancy at such an early stage should be easy. The key is to look, and act, as normal as possible. Wear as much of your regular wardrobe as you can, making small allowances for your lack of a waist by wearing longer sweaters or shirts and unbuttoning the top button of your pants. (No one will notice, I promise.) Drawstring or elastic waistbands are also great at this stage, and you could buy one or two low-waisted pants or skirts to tide you over. Just try your best to avoid any oversized items that will truly make you look much bigger than you are right now.

casual fridays

What a relief! Casual Fridays are such a break after a long week in constricting clothes. On these days when you can take it down a notch, I still encourage you to maintain a level of profession-alism. The harsh reality of pregnancy is that it doesn't take a lot to look sloppy, and at work you need to look neat and pulled together. Choose your separates wisely. Save the denim, corduroy, and active wear for the weekends. Simple skirts, tailored pants, comfortable sweaters, and broadcloth shirts are better options.

winter

spring

summer

fall

maternity
must
have:
twin set

work

first trimester

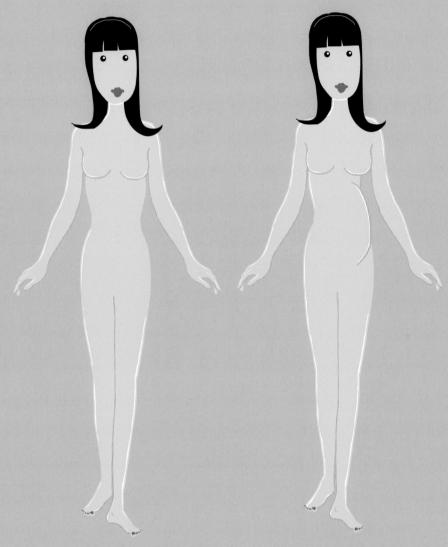

pre-pregnancy
you

1st-trimester
you

There's absolutely no reason to buy maternity clothes for your first trimester. I know it's hard. You're excited, naturally, and probably noticed almost immediately that you stopped fitting into your normal clothing. Your waist is gone, your breasts are a cup-size bigger, and even if that "pooch" is caused by digestive irregularities, it still doesn't remove the fact that half your wardrobe has been relegated to the back of the closet.

For most women, however, especially those pregnant for the first time, you really don't "pop" until your sixteenth week. This is hard to believe, I know, considering the many changes that are going on in your body, but all the doctors agree. My doctor, Laura Schiller of New York's Mt. Sinai Medical Center, says, "It takes twelve weeks for the uterus to rise out of the pelvis." You may be peeing all the time and look and feel distended and bloated, but at this stage the baby is really the size of a thimble. Your discomfort, although genuine, is caused more by hormones than actual fetal growth.

So what does that mean from a style point of view? It means that maternity clothing at this stage will only be impractical and unflattering. You will look bigger (aka fatter) if you wear an oversized maternity T-shirt at ten weeks. And since you really have no idea how big you're going to get (and you will get bigger!), it doesn't make sense to buy maternity clothes now, only to have to reinvest in larger sizes down the road.

For now, tide yourself over. Think of the first trimester as an afternoon snack and buy a small selection of inexpensive clothes in a size or two larger than normal that can take you through a couple of months. Shop at places like Target,

Express, Old Navy, Gap, or Banana Republic. Club Monaco is a good source for dressier work attire. There are any number of stores on Main Street and at the mall where you can find reasonably priced clothes that won't gouge your wallet. At the maternity stores there are below-the-belly styles that fit this transitional niche. Also remember that the clothes you buy now may come in handy in the future. Although no one likes to talk about it, it will probably take you a few months after the birth to fit back into your regular clothes. We'll discuss this in the postpartum chapter, but remind yourself of the fact that these "transitional" items may be useful again.

When shopping for these short-term additions, do try to remember that fitted really is better. Especially now when most people don't even know you're pregnant, there's no reason to raise the red flag with a shapeless tunic or extra-large shirt. In truth you only need items that are at most two sizes bigger, though this varies, of course, from top to bottom. Your best bet is to look for slightly roomier tees and blouses, and pants with low-slung waists and a stretchy fabric. There are also so many and great stretch jeans these days, and it's easy to find skirts that wrap or those that have an elastic waistband.

Have faith. The first trimester can be very hard, with the exhaustion, the nausea, and the hourly visits to the bathroom. Your changing body and shrinking wardrobe can be a source of some anxiety, even in the midst of such happiness and excitement. So many women I know describe themselves as feeling fat and unused to the way their new pregnant body feels. I, too, recall feeling huge at this stage, "but remember" my doctor told me, "this time passes quickly as the pregnancy progresses."

This is all to say that it will be easier when you really "look" pregnant. Now you really want a belly! But in the meantime, bear with your swollen breasts, wear a comfortable and supportive bra, and revel in the fact that you've got a little cleavage and can still squeeze into your favorite jeans for a little while longer.

weekends

Comfort. This is the key to your weekend wardrobe. After a long week at work, the opportunity to relax is a welcome change, and whether you're taking a nap, running errands, shopping, or spending the afternoon in the park with your kids, this is the time for you to enjoy yourself.

The clothes you choose, therefore, should embody this laid-back approach. There's no reason to fuss or overdo it on the weekends, because the beauty of American style, and especially American sportswear, is that it's so clean and casual. Now's the time to celebrate the fact that you're not constrained by office etiquette—and really let your personal style shine through.

First, consider that your weekend closet, far more than your work attire, will be informed by the seasons. This may sound like common sense, but I've divided this chapter into warm and cold weather sections so that you can plan accordingly. More than anything, versatility is important. While you're still able to flit freely from one weekend activity to another, you should choose a weekend wardrobe that can take you from mornings at home to museum afternoons.

summer lovin'

Maternity dressing is a cinch when you're pregnant in the summer. I believe it's the easiest season during which to be pregnant because it is so casual and relaxed. Your non-pregnant friends may keep asking about the humidity and the bloating and "isn't it hard carrying around all that weight in the heat?," and there certainly are drawbacks to lugging around an oversized stomach during the hottest months. But in truth (and I was pregnant with both of my children during the summer), the summer is just the simplest

SURPRISE! A HALTER PROVIDES A LOT OF SUPPORT. IT'S ADJUSTABLE AND SEXY AND GOES BEAUTIFULLY WITH SHORT SHORTS THAT SHOW OFF YOUR LEGS. A SUPER OUTFIT DAY OR NIGHT.

CAPRIS, OR CROPPED PANTS, ARE A SUMMER STAPLE. PAIR WITH A SLEEVELESS BLOUSE IN A SWEET PRINT. A LEMON YELLOW CARDIGAN (MAYBE YOU ALREADY OWN ONE?) ADDS A LITTLE PUNCH.

JEWEL TONES ARE SO PRETTY, AND THIS FLOUNCY SKIRT IS PARTICULARLY FEMININE. BALANCE THE LOOSE LINES ON THE BOTTOM WITH SOMETHING SIMPLE AND FITTED ON TOP.

season to work with from a style perspective. Throw on capris and a tee and you're ready to go—to the beach, to the store, to a backyard barbecue. There's an ease and freedom to summer dressing that's perfect for a pregnant woman. You've got enough on your mind these days, and you just don't have to give a lot of thought to your summer wardrobe. Better still, most summer outfits, especially the sundress, easily transition from day to night.

STRIPES SCREAM SUMMERTIME. AND CONTRARY TO PUBLIC OPINION, THEY DO LOOK GOOD ON A PREGNANT WOMAN. RED, WHITE, AND KHAKI ARE A CLASSIC COLOR COMBINATION.

SKIRTS ARE COMFORTABLE AND EASY WHEN IT'S HOT. CHOOSE A LIGHT, BREEZY FABRIC AND MATCH WITH A COLORFUL TEE. COMPLETE THE OUTFIT WITH A PAIR OF SIMPLE SLIDES.

maternity must have: wrap sweater

Question: It's July. My feet are swollen, my arms feel fat, and all I want to do is float in a cool pool. How can I look, and feel, good when the heat is on?
— Janice, Washington, D.C.

Answer: Nothing can redefine "hot" like being pregnant in the summer. The humidity can be particularly exhausting for a pregnant woman, especially when she's concerned about dehydration and overheating. But take heart. As hot as it is, you can look cool as a cucumber with little effort. First, choose light, airy fabrics that don't cling. Fitted is okay, but you want to avoid anything that binds too tight. If you're uncomfortable with your arms, wide-neck tanks draw attention to your neck and face but still allow you the comfort of going sleeveless. Or opt for T-shirts with sleeves that go almost to the elbow. When in doubt, bring along a cotton cardigan to tie around your neck or throw on if, luckily, it gets a little cool at night.

CALIFORNIA
DREAMIN':
MICHELLE PHILLIPS,
PREGNANT IN
DECEMBER 1967.

swimwear

If you're like me, you spend your summer weekends as close to water as possible. I love the beach and the pool, and so was appalled during my first pregnancy to find that all that was available in maternity stores were oversized froufrou grandma suits. What a joke! The suits looked like a hideous mix of Shirley Temple and Coney Island circa 1941. Unless I was going to get an audition for a part in an Esther Williams film, there was no way I was putting that on my pregnant body. So, I immediately went to Bloomingdales and bought a regular suit, just three sizes bigger. The beauty of the bathing suit, of course, is that it stretches. You really don't need to invest in a maternity suit (although the ones on the market now are far more flattering); you just need to find a style in a supportive yet not suffocating fabric. And as cute as they are, stay away from the flimsy fabrics like knits. They're sexy, sure, but won't hold you in, stretch out to a point of no return, and rarely come with that all-essential built-in bra.

A lot of pregnant women cringe at the idea of wearing a bathing suit, but honestly, most suits work well on expanding bodies. Shelf-cup bras are especially helpful, as shown here in this classic black tank.
An adjustable halter in come-hither red also provides added support and a sexy neckline. And, if you dare, take the plunge and go for a colorful bikini. This is the ultimate suit to show off your new shape in all its glory.

cover-up

This word takes on new importance when you're pregnant, especially during the summer when you want something easy to take you from the beach to a quick lunch. You want something you can throw on over a suit and look cute and put together, something that will shade you from the sun without providing head-to-toe coverage. Tunics in a fun fabric shield your shoulders, while sundresses are perfect for shopping excursions and poolside fun. My favorite cover-up, however, is a colorful *pareo* (aka sarong). This big rectangle of fabric is traditional to many cultures and absolutely ideal for pregnancy. Wrap it above or below your bump. Wear it with a bikini, a one-piece, or as a summer skirt with a bathing suit or tank as a top.

"MY HUSBAND JUST LOVED THE FACT THAT I WAS
I WAS PREGNANT, WHETHER IT WAS A BATHING SUIT ON
COTTON BLOUSE, OR AN EVENING GOWN TO THE

MODEL VALERIA MAZZA DOES IT RIGHT. ON THE BEACH IN PUNTA DEL ESTE, URUGUAY, WITH HUSBAND GRAVIER AND SON BALTHAZAR.

PREGNANT WITH HIS CHILD. I COULD WEAR ANYTHING WHEN THE BEACH IN MEXICO, CAPRI PANTS WITH A ³/₄-LENGTH ACADEMY AWARDS." — VANESSA WILLIAMS, ACTRESS/SINGER

tee time

Tees are your must-have summer staple. They go with everything: shorts, skirts, capris, slim-fitting pants, and now they're even better for expecting mothers because they have a little stretch. Today's styles tend to be shorter and more fitted than the traditional trapeze (i.e., "oversized") shirt, which makes them eminently more flattering. They also come in a variety of necklines and sleeve lengths, and some even have that convenient built-in bra. During the summer, and throughout your pregnancy, T-shirts should be a basic underpinning of your wardrobe.

Pick a color, any color.
CLOCKWISE FROM TOP:
RUSCHED ¾ SLEEVE,
LONG-SLEEVE CREWNECK,
DRESSY TANK,
LONG-SLEEVE V-NECK,
SLEEVELESS CROSS-OVER,
KEY NECK A-LINE.

With the coming of fall and winter, your weekend wardrobe changes. A whole new range of fabrics and colors enter the equation, and with that a cozy approach that accommodates the changing weather. Perhaps it's that left-over back-to-school feeling, but the fall is always an exciting time to restock your closet and hunker down for the cool months to come. The great, and economical, thing about your winter weekend wardrobe is that there's loads of cross-over with work attire. The sweaters you selected to go with a suit can easily be worn with casual pants for a dressed-down look. Or those cigarette pants you bought for a more casual Friday can now find new life with a whimsical blouse. Just be creative. Where summer has ease, winter has economy. With a little help and a little imagination you can easily reconfigure a weekend closet.

CHYNNA PHILLIPS GETS IT RIGHT WITH A CLEAN, MORE
TAILORED VARIATION ON HUSBAND WILLIAM BALDWIN'S CLOSET.

ON-THE-STREET CHIC. LOOKS LIKE CINDY CRAWFORD AND HUSBAND
RANDE GERBER ARE SHOPPING FOR TRANSITIONAL CLOTHES.

layering

When you're pregnant it can often feel like a little oven is burning inside you. This wasn't supposed to happen until menopause, you say, but when the hot flashes come and sweat starts pooling under your collar and breasts, you realize that one of the unspoken side effects of pregnancy is the ability to stay warm no matter how frigid it is—in or out of doors. The answer, of course, is to layer. During any sea-

"I BASE MY FASHION TASTE ON WHAT

son, my advice is to start with a T-shirt, then add a blouse or shirt, and on top of that a sweater. Twin sets are stellar variations on this theme. Just build as you need to, and give yourself every opportunity to strip down and peel off. Keep in mind those over air-conditioned stores and restaurants in summer. Also remember that pregnant skin is extra sensitive and you need something soft next to you.

DOESN'T ITCH." – GILDA RADNER

"WITH MY SECOND BABY,
I WAS LUCKY TO BE PREGNANT
THROUGH THE WINTER, WHICH
IS MUCH EASIER. SWEATERS
SAVED ME, AND A PAIR
OF MEN'S JEANS THAT I WORE
VERY LOW ON MY HIPS.
I FOUND I WAS MORE
COMFORTABLE WITHOUT
ANYTHING CONSTRICTING MY
BELLY. IF I HAD TO DRESS
UP, I LOVED VERY SIMPLE,
STREAMLINED DRESSES THAT
HAD A SLIM CUT SO YOU
COULD SEE THE PREGNANCY,
NOT A LOT OF BULK."
— JULIANNE MOORE, ACTRESS

NEW

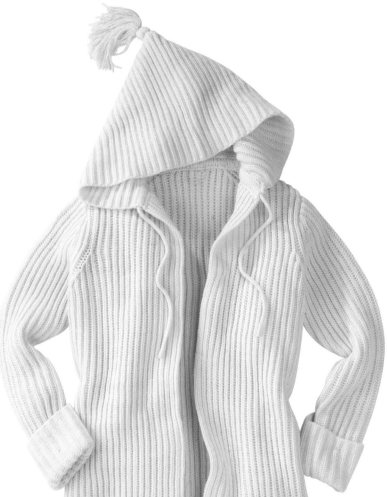

over the top

Like the summer tee, the weekend sweater is your go-to item. Select from any number of styles—turtlenecks, crewnecks, V-necks—and pair them with pants or skirts to create the optimum number of looks. Wool and cotton blends, superfine merinos, and especially cashmere are great and not as itchy as traditional Shetland wools. Good sweaters can be expensive, so the key is to select only a few fantastic pieces. At the end of my second pregnancy, I lived in a black turtleneck. I often paired it with a black pair of pants, and the outfit was simple, monochromatic, and easy to get into. I always felt pulled together, and best of all the ensemble transitioned perfectly from afternoon errands to a laid-back dinner with friends.

Anything goes!
CHOOSE YOUR FAVORITE
SHAPE AND WEIGHT.
CLOCKWISE FROM TOP:
SWEATER JACKET,
DRESSY KNIT,
BOYFRIEND SWEATER,
FISHERMAN SWEATER,
BASIC BLACK TURTLENECK.

bottoms up

Pants are the most basic component of your fall and winter wardrobe. They are the foundation from which you'll build any outfit, and with the variety of fabrics and styles available today, your choices are truly endless. Fabricwise,

I particularly like corduroy and suede (often made of a more affordable stretch synthetic), both of which are classic weekend looks. Better designers now create pants without the front or side panels traditionally available in

stretch corduroy   **stretch hi-tech**   **stretch wool**   **stretch leather**

"ON THE WEEKENDS, MY UNIFORM CONSISTED OF A
LOOKED GOOD AND HIP AND MADE ME FEEL CUTE,

most maternity stores. Instead of panels, they use fabrics that incorporate a healthy amount of stretch and can therefore grow with you, offering a smoother look and at the same time allowing you to wear shorter, more stylish tops.

Also popular these days are below-the-belly styles. Although they require slightly longer shirts and sweaters, many women find them more comfortable and more in keeping with their pre-pregnancy look.

stretch below-the-belly

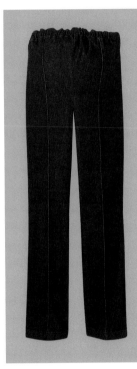

denim

Denim should almost have a chapter unto itself. It is so versatile and such a great weekend wardrobe staple season after season. Truly one of the backbones of American sportswear, denim now comes in so many different colors, rinses, weights, and styles. There are wonderful stretchy options when you're pregnant, and beyond jeans there are skirts and jackets, and even dressier denim, too.

CASHMERE TUBE TOP AND LEATHER PANTS. IT ALWAYS WHICH IS SO IMPORTANT WHEN YOU ARE PREGNANT."
— LISA RINNA, ACTRESS

Coats

There's no reason to buy a new coat when you are pregnant. This is an investment you absolutely do not have to make, considering you'll be hugely pregnant for a single season at most. It certainly isn't a crime to leave your current coat unbuttoned, and chances are you'll be warm (and layered!) anyway, so leaving your coat open won't do you any harm. Wraps and shawls over your coat can help keep you warm on extremely frigid days. But if you must invest, styles I like include car coats, pea coats, and stylish parkas. One of my favorite looks is a short swing coat, which is equally accessible for weekends or work. But, and I repeat, unless the only coat in your closet is a fitted princess style, you should be able to get away with what you already own.

NICOLE AND EDDIE MURPHY

CATE BLANCHETT.

AERIN LAUDER

ELLE MACPHERSON

JODIE FOSTER

KIMORA LEE SIMMONS

THE MILLER SISTERS

LUCIE DE LA FALAISE

JAMELIA

BERNADETTE AND
SUGAR RAY LEONARD

MARIA BELLO

"PREGNANT MOTHER AND DAUGHTER IN HYDE PARK." MAY 1959.

Walking. Stretching. Yoga. Tennis.
Every pregnancy book you
read exalts the benefits of exercise during
pregnancy, and all of these activities
are excellent ways to stay fit and
prepare your mind and body for the big
event to come. The uterus
may be the strongest muscle in a woman's
body, but it takes more than
strength to push a baby out. It takes
stamina, patience, and a lot of flexibility.
The instructor in your birthing
class wasn't joking when she said the
baby's head comes out there.
Yes, somehow at the end of all this you
will push a seven-poundish baby
out of your birth canal. If that doesn't
require a little advance preparation,
and perhaps a little exercise, I don't
know what does.

weekends

"WALKING WAS THE ONE ACTIVITY THAT MADE FROM SWELLING, KEPT MY WEIGHT WITHIN

active attire

Most workout wear is by nature designed to be stretchy. This is obviously a good thing when you're pregnant, and it means that during your first few months you can probably get away with the same gear that you usually wear. The bigger you get, however, the more constricting that waistband will become. Sometime around month five you'll need to think about apparel specifically designed for your bulging belly. Now is the time to pack away your T-shirts and leggings. Whether you hit the track or the treadmill for five or fifty minutes, you can now do so without your tummy hanging out.

ME FEEL BETTER—IT KEPT MY FEET AND HANDS
REASON, AND MADE ME FEEL RELAXED."
– JULIANNE MOORE

The happy fact is that it's easier than ever before for moms-to-be to exercise in style. Many big-name athletic companies have finally recognized that pregnant women are viable consumers, and now there are active wear lines designed exclusively for maternity. Stretch pants with supportive panels, exercise bras, comfy yoga pants, and cat suits have all been created with a pregnant woman's growing needs in mind. Keeping an expectant mother dry and cool is also important, and many designs today use state-of-the-art moisture-management fabrics that let your busy body breathe.

prenatal fitness

These days, everyone believes in prenatal fitness.
content to lie around the house (often with a
other), but today, woman are encouraged to get
half an hour of walking each day does wonders
is to choose the exercise that is right for you.
practice, so if you've never set foot on a track
day—no matter how worried you are about
gentle, low-impact, and works to increase your
option, as are the treadmill and elliptical trainer
getting yourself to a gym, much less onto any
That's fine, and on those days I recommend
and a pint of frozen yogurt. Sometimes when
siren song of Ben & Jerry's calling to you from
to treat yourself, and if that means an afternoon

When our mothers were pregnant they were
cigarette in one hand and a martini in the
up, get out, and get themselves moving. Even a
toward keeping you in shape. My best advice
Pregnancy is not a time to take up a rigorous
in your life, don't start running three miles a
gaining weight. Choose an activity that is
strength and flexibility. Yoga is an excellent
at your gym. Certainly there will be days when
machine, seems overwhelming and exhausting.
nothing more than a couch, a remote control,
you're pregnant all you want to hear is the
the freezer. And that's fine. Pregnancy is a time
of cookies 'n cream, then go for it!

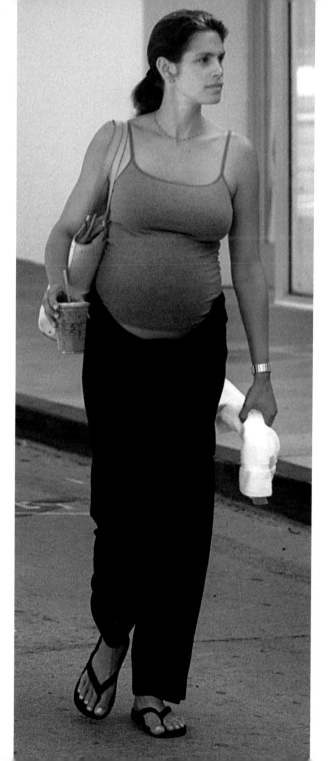

from the gym to the street

Sometimes it seems that active wear is everywhere. In the past few years workout clothing has really crossed over into regular sportswear, and this fusion of exercise apparel and everyday fashion is a great, fun look for weekend and leisure dressing. Beyond fleece, which is a wonderful cover-up, there are a variety of microfiber pants and tees that can be very chic and perfect for shopping or a quick trip to the gym. Easy to wash and even easier to wear, they are also ideal outfits for stay-at-home moms, who when pregnant with a second (or third) child, keenly understand the need for easy-on, easy-off attire.

The shoe, of course, for this on-the-go look is a colorful athletic shoe. Now a leading choice in casual footwear, trainers, as the fashionistas call them, have come a long way from white leather sneakers. Today's styles range from running shoes and cross-trainers to retro skateboarding and tennis varieties that are not only hip but, better yet, comfortable. I know many women today who have adopted their trainers as an essential part of their daily wardrobe.

Question: At 36 weeks, all I want is to be comfortable. I know it's unflattering, but I can't seem to tear myself away from leggings and my husband's shirt. Any suggestions for a more polished and less triangular look?
– Abigail, Boston, MA

Answer: With one month to go, by all means be as comfortable as possible. The ubiquitous leggings and an oversized shirt are an old pregnancy standby for good reason, but if you're looking to update things a bit, try a flare-bottom pant instead of the old tight-around-the-ankle variety. That passé style only makes you look enormous on top, while the new cut stresses better proportions and presents a vastly more modern silhouette. Stick with your husband's shirts around the house, but if you're going out, pair the leggings with a loose-fitting top.

1

FLEECE IS WARM, COZY, AND A BEST-BET COVER-UP FOR COOL WINTER EVENINGS.

2

THE MAN'S-STYLE SHIRT. AT HOME YOU CAN WEAR IT AS BIG AND BAGGY AS YOU LIKE.

3

A TANK IS THE COOLEST— AND SEXIEST—TOP TO WEAR WHILE LOLLING ON THE COUCH.

4

GET COMFORTABLE IN LOOSE-FITTING YOGA PANTS. MY NIGHTLY STAPLE.

5

AH, DENIM. FIND A PAIR THAT'S AS SOFT AND WORN IN AS POSSIBLE.

3 + 4 = breakfast in bed

3 + 5 = movie night

2 + 5 = sit down to dinner

m
mix
+
m
match

lounging at home

At the end of a long day, there's nothing better than slipping into comfy clothes to lounge around the house. Get out of those waist-constricting pants and ankle-suffocating socks and slip into something soft, loose, and, if you can muster up the energy, sexy. Leisure wear need not be an old pair of sweats and an oversized tee. There are eminently more attractive, and equally comfortable, options. When I was pregnant, I lived in a pair of drawstring pajama pants, stretch camisole, and cozy cashmere cardigan. Soft tanks, flare-bottom stretch pants, and roomy button-down shirts are other ideas that can stylishly take you through hours of television or chapters of *What to Expect When You're Expecting.*

**2 + 4 =
household
chores**

**1 + 5 =
morning
coffee**

**1 + 4 =
Sunday-night
tv**

intimate apparel

They may not show, but bras and underwear are the most essential components of your wardrobe. Perhaps it's because they are one of the first things to change when we get pregnant, but most expecting women I know are obsessed with their breasts. How big will they get? Are they going to sag? What will they look like when all this is done? A healthy amount of cleavage now may be a welcome change, but the idea of looking like a *National Geographic* photograph in the future isn't. Invest in a supportive bra. Go to a department store and lock yourself in a room with one of the helpful saleswomen. As humiliating as it sounds to have a stranger pawing at your breasts, these women really know their stuff and can help you select a style that will help you keep your breasts your breasts.

As for underwear, this is another area worthy of debate. Many maternity stores carry the oversized grandma variety that come up high over your belly. Theoretically this is a good idea and prevents things like unattractive panty lines. In reality, however, most women I've met aren't big fans of this style, and opt for something that fits under the belly. This could mean a thong, a bikini, or even a G-string. Just buy a size (or two) up and stay away from anything too hip-hugging or tight. *Loose* is the byword for maternity underwear. The last thing you need is an enormous pair of panties binding you in.

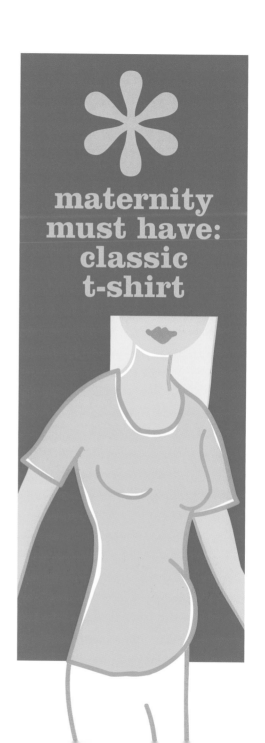

maternity
must have:
classic
t-shirt

"AS I PUT ON MY ENTIRE RECOMMENDED WEIGHT GAIN IN MY FIRST TRIMESTER—GRADUALLY BALLOONING UNTIL I ULTIMATELY GAINED SIXTY (60!) POUNDS—FITTED CLOTHES WERE HARDLY AN OPTION. MY WARDROBE WAS BASICALLY BAGGY, BAGGIER, AND BAGGIEST. AROUND THE FORTY-POUND MARK, PEOPLE BEGAN TELLING ME I LOOKED 'RADIANT,' WHICH, BASICALLY, I BELIEVE MEANS, 'BOY, ARE YOU FAT!' AT THE FIFTY-POUND MARK, PEOPLE WHO HADN'T SEEN ME IN A WHILE WOULD TAKE ONE LOOK AND BURST OUT LAUGHING. AT THE FINAL SIXTY-POUND MARK, TWO WEEKS OVERDUE, I WAS WADDLING THROUGH BERGDORF'S AND NOTICED A WOMAN STARING AT ME. AFTER SEVERAL MINUTES, SHE CAME OVER TO ME AND SAID, 'YOU KNOW, YOU HAVE CANDICE BERGEN'S FACE.'"

— CANDICE BERGEN, ACTRESS

second trimester

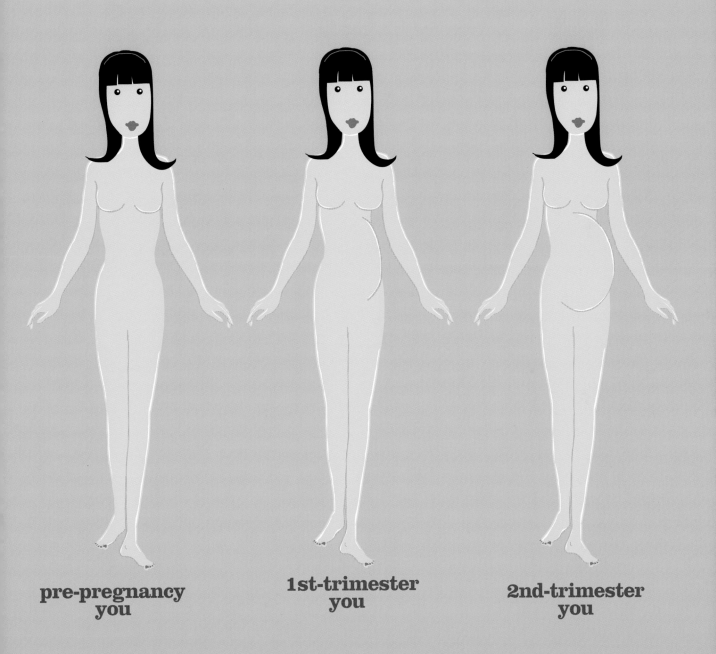

pre-pregnancy
you

1st-trimester
you

2nd-trimester
you

Enjoy it. Your second trimester is by far the best stage of pregnancy for most women. Almost overnight it seems that your nausea subsides, your energy returns, and sometime around your twentieth week you are big enough to look adorably pregnant and not just suspiciously fat. This is also the time when you can begin to feel the baby move. The realization that you're actually carrying something inside you, that it's not a trick of the sonogram or a figment of your very active imagination, is incredibly powerful. For many, this is when you finally get it: Yes, you really are pregnant!

In truth, your second trimester is what this book is about, because now you can start thinking about maternity wear. When you're feeling better, you want to look better, and chances are you've started to show. It happens to some women earlier than others (if it's your second pregnancy it could be as early as 10 or 12 weeks), but when it does happen it seems to happen overnight. You wake up one day and there's the bump. "By the beginning of the second trimester," Dr. Schiller says, "the fetus is four inches long and weighs about an ounce." That's not very big, you say, but the second trimester is a period of enormous growth. What started out as a string bean soon becomes a serious force. And although every woman carries differently, Dr. Schiller says that by the end of the second trimester the fetus has typically grown to 14 inches and weighs 2$\frac{1}{2}$ pounds.

But let's not get ahead of ourselves. Let's begin slowly and think of dressing for pregnancy like learning to swim (which is not a bad metaphor, really, considering what's going on inside of you). Your first assignment is to learn to tread water. By this I mean survey your options and do a little research. Talk to your friends, go online, take a reconnaissance trip to a maternity store at the mall. There are so many maternity wear shops now, from huge national chains like Target to smaller boutique stores. It will really behoove you to do a little exploration before you start to buy because many lines carry similar items, and the range of prices can vary widely.

Economy, of course, is a big concern when you're pregnant, and it's during your second trimester that these "real life" worries begin to set in. How are you going to afford this baby anyway? That's a genuine question when not too shortly down the road you're going to need to invest in a stroller, a crib, a changing table, and toys. The list can seem endless, but when you're literally bursting out of the pants that fit you just a week ago, your first order of business is maternity clothes.

So before you buy, assess your lifestyle and where you want to spend. If you work in a professional environment, you'll probably want to invest in high-quality office wear and simply supplement those items with a couple of inexpensive tees, shirts, and a pair of jeans for your weekends. Or if you're a stay-at-home mom, you may find inexpensive items for everyday and instead splurge on a couple of knockout outfits for the evening. Only you can determine what's right for your lifestyle. Just take the time to think before you buy. Maternity clothes can be expensive, and you'll want to consider your many options before you whip out your credit card.

When you are ready to buy, take full advantage of the sales staff at the store. They really know what they're doing and can be incredibly helpful. They can also help you manipulate those funny little tummy pillows in the dressing room. We use them in my store, and they really do help you envision how big you're going to be and how much space you need to account for. Because the bottom line is, if you shop right, you shouldn't have to trade up for larger clothes in your final months. The clothes you buy now should last you throughout the rest of your pregnancy (save, perhaps, your final few weeks).

If you're shopping online, which is increasingly common these days, it's a little more difficult to tell if those pants have enough wiggle room or if they're going to be skin tight in your sixth month. Be careful. Buy stretch fabrics, and as soon as they arrive in the mail, make sure you have a couple of good inches in the waist (if it's too big now, you can always just roll a waistband down). Virtually every online retailer lets you send anything back that doesn't fit, so shop away. This is the best part of your pregnancy—and you deserve to look fabulous.

evenings

Admit it. As soon as you discovered you were pregnant, you immediately checked your calendar to see how many evening events you had to attend over the next nine months. Somehow, the dreaded words "black tie" send every pregnant woman into a panicked frenzy, rifling through her closet, tossing clothes on the bed, searching for the perfect outfit, only to realize that there's no way that cute halter dress will ever fit two months from now.

Getting dressed up, even when you're not pregnant, can be scary; when you're carrying around twenty pounds of extra weight it can be downright terrifying. We all want to look our best, to impress our friends, our clients, our husband's boss. We want everyone to say, "Wow. You look amazing." Because even if we don't feel amazing, we still want everyone to believe that we do.

The good news is that it's actually pretty easy. And, surprise, even economical. You don't have to spend a lot of money to look good at night, and with a little mixing and matching, a little bare shoulder here and a little cover-up there, evening dressing can be the perfect opportunity to shine. A night out on the town, an evening at the opera, a charity ball, or a high school reunion are all great excuses to have some fun. So relax: you can do this.

Stepping Out
TOP ROW:
ACTRESS/MODEL OLATZ
SCHNABEL WITH ARTIST
JULIAN SCHNABEL, JADA
PINKETT, UMA THURMAN,
THANDIE NEWTON.
BOTTOM ROW:
STEPHANIE SEYMOUR,
MODEL LILI MALTESE,
SOCIALITE RENE
ROCKEFELLER,
JULIANNE MOORE,
JANE LEEVES.

LEFT TO RIGHT TOP: JOHN SPELLMAN/RETNA LTD; OSCAR/RETNA LTD; CHARLES SYKES/REX USA; ALAN DAVIDSON/RETNA LTD; BOTTOM: WALTER McBRIDE /RETNA LTD; DAVID FISHER/LFI; MARY HILLIARD; BRENDA CHASE/ONLINE/GETTY IMAGES; PAUL ANDREWS/BIG PICTURES USA.

I don't believe in rules
when it comes to maternity dressing.
But when it comes to evenings, I definitely
have some advice. First of all, wear what
makes you feel the most beautiful—and
comfortable. You know your body better
than anyone else, and if you sailed down
the red carpet in a slip dress before you
were pregnant, chances are you can pull it
off now. When it comes to an evening
wardrobe, the most important thing to
remember is that you, not your clothes,
should stand out. Beautiful cuts and colors
are immune to fashion trends, and
elegance is always in. Above all, try
not to forget that feeling sexy and sensual
is what pregnancy is all about. Correct
me if I'm wrong, but isn't sex how you got
here in the first place?

dress down

The first thing to remember when getting ready at night is: you don't need to be the dressiest person in the room. Even when I'm not pregnant, I strongly believe that understated is the best way to go. Unless it's your birthday party or a benefit for which you're the co-chair, there's no need to pull out every stop. Less is definitely more. Our mothers told us this first, while wiping off that high school makeup, and as much as we hate to admit they're right, it's really true. It's also true that ball gowns are just not flattering on a pregnant woman. If Grace Kelly couldn't wear the New Look at nine months, then neither can you. Too much fabric and volume will only make you look bigger than you are, and as much as I stand behind celebrating your new body, that doesn't mean showing it off in unflattering ways. Instead of pleats and bustles, go for something sleek and classic, concentrating on clean lines and quality fabrics.

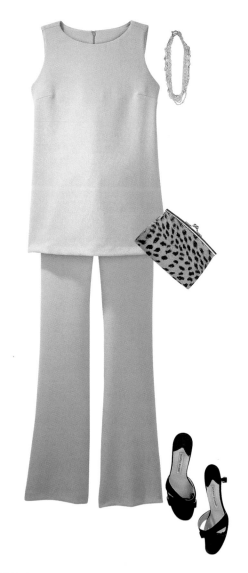

A SOPHISTICATED PANTS SUIT IS STREAMLINED AND MODERN. SELECT A SEXY EVENING FABRIC IN A LIGHT COLOR FOR THE ADDED IMPACT YOU WANT AT NIGHT. A LITTLE LEOPARD PURSE IS A GREAT TOUCH, AS ARE OPEN-TOED SHOES (DON'T FORGET THE PEDICURE!).

Accessories
Jewelry can be incredibly strategic. Some people say it draws attention to your face, but I tend to think it lures the eyes a little lower. Like the old adage says: If you've got it, flaunt it.

A SIMPLE, SLINKY DRESS IS ONE OF MY FAVORITES. THIS ONE HAS A PRETTY COWL NECK AND SOFT, FLUID LINES. DEPENDING ON THE OCCASION, IT COULD EASILY BE DRESSED DOWN OR UP AS IT IS HERE WITH A SHIMMERY WRAP. GREAT FOR A DINNER DATE OR BLACK-TIE AFFAIR.

1

A BLACK JERSEY V-NECK
IS A BLANK CANVAS,
EASILY DRESSED UP OR
DRESSED DOWN.

2

A CHOCOLATE BROWN
CARDIGAN, AGAIN IN
MATTE JERSEY, IS RICH
AND SUPPLE.

3

CAMEL IS A FLAWLESS
NEUTRAL—COOL,
CLASSIC, AND COZY IN
A SOFT KNIT.

4

FUN AND FLIRTY—
A BLACK MATTE
JERSEY SKIRT.

5

AN ALL-AROUND
FAVORITE. PULL-ON
MATTE JERSEY
PANTS IN BLACK.

**1 + 4 =
romantic
dinner date**

**1 + 5 =
saturday-night
movie**

**3 + 4 =
gallery opening**

a separate piece

Separates are fabulous. Not only are they chic, they can save you money. Separates allow you to repurpose clothes you already own, and my first advice to clients who need help with an evening outfit is to tell them to look in their closets. Because, really, how many times are you going to wear a dressy maternity outfit? Unless you're a Hollywood starlet, probably not too often.

**3 + 5 =
entertaining
at home**

**2 + 3 + 5 =
happy hour**

**2 + 5 =
business
function**

"I ALWAYS KEPT IT VERY SIMPLE, WHICH, THANKFULLY, IS WHAT MY HUSBAND PREFERRED. WHY OVERTLY SEX IT UP? YOU'VE ALREADY PROVEN YOUR ABILITY TO ATTRACT SOMEONE."

— JESSICA SEINFELD, FOUNDER OF BABY BUGGY CHARITY

"I COULDN'T LIVE WITHOUT A PULL-ON PAIR OF BLACK JERSEY PANTS. I WORE THEM ON AND OFF THE SET OF *THE PRACTICE.* THEY WERE MY ALL-TIME FAVORITE THROUGHOUT MY PREGNANCY!"

— KELLI WILLIAMS, ACTRESS

maternity must have: black pants

basic black

Black, of course, is always key. You've known since your first issue of *Seventeen* that black is slimming. It's also smart, seasonless, and goes with everything. I always tell my clients that if you plan on purchasing one dressy piece while you're pregnant, go for something black. A long black skirt, a sleeveless sweater, and of course a ubiquitous little (or not so little!) black dress. Coco Chanel was right when she said every woman needs a little black dress. Black takes you anywhere, day to night. It's appropriate for a work-related cocktail party, looks fabulous at a play, and with a strand of pearls can take you to a fundraiser. Even if you go out a lot at night and want more variety in your evening wardrobe, black is still the perfect base.

LEFT TO RIGHT: IMAN IS A PERFECT LADY IN A LONG BROCADE DRESS COAT. CAROLYN MURPHY TAKES OUR BREATH AWAY IN THIS SHEER BLACK DRESS. UMA THURMAN IS COOL AND CLASSIC AS ALWAYS.

spot of color

Bold, beautiful colors bring any evening outfit to life. Building on your basic black components, you can easily create a dazzling look geared toward any kind of affair, whether an after-work event or a gala ball. You'll be surprised, I think, by the number of options you hadn't considered. Even the simplest sweater can be dressed up with the right skirt and accessories, and you'll see that good taste is really just the combination of grace and attitude.

A CLASSIC BLACK AND WHITE HOUNDSTOOTH TAKES YOU ANYWHERE, DAY TO NIGHT. PAIR IT WITH A TWIN SET IN CASHMERE OR MERINO.

TUBE TOPS LOOK GREAT ON ALMOST ANYONE. TRUST ME. TRY IT IN A VARYING WIDTH STRIPE WITH A SLIM PAIR OF DRESSY BLACK PANTS.

"DON'T GIVE A WOMAN ADVICE. ONE SHOULD NEVER GIVE A WOMAN ANYTHING SHE CAN'T WEAR IN THE EVENING."
— OSCAR WILDE

PARTNER A BLACK SHELL WITH A SHIMMERY SKIRT IN AN UNEXPECTED COLOR. THE HI/LOW CONTRAST POPS, AND THE SWEATER'S ADDED DETAILS ARE A LOVELY TOUCH.

THE PERFECT OFFICE-TO-EVENING ENSEMBLE. A SIMPLE SWEATER IN A BRIGHT JEWEL TONE PERKS UP A PENCIL SKIRT AND MATCHING JACKET. ADD SIMPLE, SLING-BACK HEELS.

The wrap dress is a classic.
Originated by
Diane von Furstenberg during the
seventies and revived to
great acclaim during the nineties,
it is now a fashion fundamental
and one that should be
a staple in any pregnant woman's
closet. Not only is the wrap
inherently adjustable,
but its soft lines and slim-fitting
bodice are particularly flattering
on an expectant figure.
Every season I include a wrap
dress in my line and find
that they transition perfectly from
daytime to evening.

glamorama

Most women, myself included, tend to splurge for evening clothes. Even if you spend most nights at home with your husband, you still want to look like a knockout when you go out on the town. But when you're pregnant, and your body is changing so quickly, it's nearly impossible, and far too expensive, to purchase a complete maternity wardrobe for evening. You really want to choose one or two special pieces to invest in. Chances are your closet already holds the foundation to a fabulous outfit, and that means you can put your money toward an extravagant piece or two without feeling a lot of guilt.

SPLURGE!   **SPLURGE!**

SAVE!   **SAVE!**   **SAVE!**   **SAVE!**

TREAT YOURSELF TO AN ANIMAL PRINT. THIS PERENNIAL TREND IS FUN AND EDGY AND SURE TO GET YOU NOTICED. PAIR WITH A BRIGHT RED TWIN SET OR A BLACK SLEEVELESS TURTLENECK, GREAT STAPLES FOR ALMOST EVERYONE'S CLOSET.

WHAT COULD BE MORE OF AN INDULGENCE THAN A ONE-SHOULDER LACE BLOUSE? IN SOFT IVORY, IT'S BOTH PROVOCATIVE AND POLISHED. FOR SPECIAL OCCASIONS ONLY, IT WILL EASILY TURN UP THE VOLUME ON BLACK PANTS OR A LONG BLACK SKIRT.

feet first

Obviously, there should be a proportional relationship between the size of your belly and the height of your heels.
Before your pregnancy you may have skipped around town in your stilettos, but now you find yourself looking longingly at flats and sensible stack heels. For evening, however, we all sacrifice a little comfort in the name of fashion. If you can stand it, go for some heel; a low pump or a strappy sandal are my favorites.
Sling backs are also very now. Think about your feet the same way as you do your body: get the courage to show some skin. Open toes are always sexier than a pump. And as long as the shape is right, evening shoes don't need to be in silk or satin. Black suede or plain leather can work just fine.

it's a wrap

A wrap is a pregnant woman's best ally. If there's one must-have accessory for evenings, it's a fabulous wrap. So many women tell me how uncomfortable they feel about their arms while they're pregnant, and a wrap allows you to go sleeveless and at the same time feel comfortably covered up. If you want to really treat yourself, match the fabric of your dress with a made-to-order wrap. I especially like fabrics that are a little sheer. With the gossamer approach you achieve a camouflage effect without sacrificing a little allure. Perhaps by the end of the evening you may even feel confident enough to leave your wrap on the back of your chair.

Question: I'm a stay-at-home mom who usually wears jeans and a T-shirt. This spring, my husband's company is throwing a huge anniversary party and I'll be eight months pregnant. Can you help?
— Sarah, Atlanta, GA

Answer: One of my favorite spring looks is a little A-line shift dress. In my store I make them in brightly colored silk shantung, and when paired with a matching coat of the same length it looks exactly like something Jackie Kennedy would have worn. The jacket will give you a little extra coverage, and the style is perfect for any special occasion.

skin deep

As you may have gathered by now, I like a woman to show a little skin at night. It's sexy. It separates day from night, and best of all, it allows you to accentuate body parts such as your arms, legs, and breasts. Although I'm not recommending you act as though you're Jayne Mansfield, there's no denying that a little cleavage can go a long way—especially for women who were less endowed prior to their pregnancies. Just ask your husband. It hasn't escaped my attention that the men who shop with their wives definitely tend to direct them toward something sexier and more revealing.

A TANKINI TOP ALLOWS YOU TO GO COMPLETELY BARE IN BACK. KEEP IT STRAIGHTFORWARD ON THE BOTTOM WITH A PAIR OF BLACK CIGARETTE PANTS. KELLY RIPA WORE THIS GUTSY KNOCKOUT TO THE EMMY'S AT 7½ MONTHS!

ANOTHER SHOULDER-BARING STYLE. THIS EMPIRE-LINE TUBE TOP HAS BONED SIDES FOR SUPPORT AND A DELICATE EYELET PATTERN FOR ADDED EMPHASIS. WHITE FLARES COMPLETE THE OUTFIT WITHOUT UPSTAGING THE TOP.

"DURING MY TWO PREGNANCIES, THE ONLY THREE PLACES MY HEAD. SO, FINE TAILORED BUTTON DOWN SHIRTS THAT OPEN AT THE NECK, SEEMED TO DO THE EVERYDAY TRICK. DRESS OR SWEATER THAT WRAPPED SNUGLY AROUND MY

THE STRAPLESS DRESS IS A CLASSIC AND LOOKS GREAT ON MANY PREGNANT WOMEN. IN A TIGHT, STRETCHY FABRIC IT ACCENTUATES YOUR BREASTS AND CALLS ATTENTION TO YOUR GROWING BELLY. IN DARING RED, IT SCREAMS: LOOK AT ME.

HALTER TOPS ARE ALL ABOUT YOUR BREASTS. AND NOW THANKS TO BUILT-IN SHELF BRAS, THEY'RE ALSO A CINCH TO WEAR, MAKING THEM ONE OF THE MOST POPULAR ITEMS I SELL. PARTNER WITH A SHORT, FLOUNCY SKIRT IN TAFFETA THAT ALSO SHOWS OFF YOUR LEGS.

AN OFF-THE-SHOULDER NECKLINE ACCENTUATES AND LENGTHENS YOUR NECK AND PLAYS UP YOUR DÉCOL-LETAGE WITHOUT EXPOSING TOO MUCH. A SEQUIN SKIRT MAKES THIS OUTFIT SOMETHING SPECIAL. FOR A DRESSY EVENING EVENT, IT'S A SHOW-STOPPER.

THAT HADN'T "WIDENED" WERE MY NECK, WRISTS, AND THE TOP OF TAPERED DOWN TO MY WRITSTS, WITH COLLARS THAT LAY WIDE THEN, IRONICALLY, WHEN I WANTED TO FEEL SEXY, I LOVED A BELLY AND SHOWED IT OFF!" –TEA LEONI DUCHOVNY, ACTRESS

in the media

When moving pictures were still silent pictures, most mentions of pregnancy were quaintly concealed behind closed doors. Even into the Technicolor era when bold epics commanded the screen, pregnancy was usually relegated to off-screen or subtle insinuations. Think of Scarlett O'Hara in *Gone with the Wind,* glamorously decked out in her long velvet robes. Now does she look pregnant? No more than poor, unlucky Melanie who keeps her agonizing delivery confined to an upstairs bedroom while Prissy, her maid, hysterically runs up and down the stairs. "Lordy," she screams, searching for hot water and towels, "I don't know nuthin' 'bout birthin' babies!" And in fact that's a pretty good metaphor for the early Hollywood system altogether.

I LOVE LUCY, 1952

FATHER'S LITTLE DIVIDEND, 1951

ALL IN THE FAMILY, 1975

FUNNY GIRL, 1968

BEWITCHED, 1969

HAIR, 1979

Pregnancy and childbirth, at least as far as Hollywood was concerned, were either a tragic

affliction (see Melanie), a phase to be ignored (how did Mary bear all those children in *It's a Wonderful Life*?), or a comedic predicament worthy of exploiting. The natural jitters and nerves of pregnancy and childbirth are ready fodder for humor, and in its own inimitable way, Hollywood soon got wise and took them for all their worth. Take *Father's Little Dividend* as an example. In this, the 1951 sequel to the equally amusing *Father of the Bride*, Elizabeth Taylor plays Kay, Spencer Tracy's adoring daughter. Gracefully gliding through pregnancy with a nipped-in waist and doleful eyes, she easily survives her arduous nine months with a minimum of grief. In an era when husbands and wives slept in separate beds (it's a wonder anyone got pregnant in the first place!), the most trying experience Daddy's little girl had to contend with was negotiating the waters of overzealous grandparents.

Throughout the decade, save perhaps Kim Hunter's portrayal of Stella in *A Streetcar Named*

Desire, portrayals of pregnancy rested firmly in the wholesome zone. These were the days of Doris Day, of Gene Kelly musicals, and Audrey Hepburn the ingenue. Post-war America was celebrating a feel-good era and any representations of pregnancy in the media were very much in keeping with that spirit. Even on the wildly popular morning news show *Today*, the deftly dressed *Today* girls, including American beauty queen Lee Meriwether and soon-to-be Brady mom Florence Henderson, were forced to disguise their pregnancies on the air. Supposedly Florence Henderson even received hate mail from angry viewers who took offense at her expectant state.

And then there was Lucy. Gloriously and obviously pregnant for all to see. When the famous

1952 episode "Lucy Is Enceinte" aired, it was the first time pregnancy was announced on television, and even then, the word "pregnant" couldn't actually be used on the air. "Expecting," "with child," "in a delicate state"—those were the euphemisms used to describe the fact that Lucy was knocked up, which came as no surprise to her loyal viewers, who for weeks had watched her disguise herself behind tent-like coats and smocks. By the time the episode finally aired on December 8, Lucille herself was very pregnant. So far along in fact that her pregnancy on the show lasted only a mere six weeks. Six weeks, however, were long enough to generate phenomenal public interest, and when "Lucy Goes to the Hospital" aired on January 18, 1953, and Little Ricky was finally delivered, it garnered an astounding 71.7 rating, which topped even the viewership of Eisenhower's inauguration.

Pregnancy, it would seem, was a hit on the air. Lucy should have been

a watershed, but in actuality it took the networks a little while to catch on. The sixties produced *Bewitched* and a pregnant Samantha did look amazing in her short shift dresses, but it wasn't really until *Rosemary's Baby* in 1968 that Hollywood started to get a little real. Granted, films don't have squeamish advertisers to contend with and Roman Polanski was the director, but this was one of the first times on the big screen where pregnancy was honestly depicted. Or as honestly as one can depict pregnancy when the mother is carrying the Devil's child. Mia Farrow, also gorgeous sporting the fashionable minis of the day, played Rosemary Woodhouse, a young pregnant housewife whose discomfort, confusion, and excitement from conception to birth all come off as incredibly real.

Equally realistic, but in their own grab-a-laugh-where-you-can ways, were the popular sitcoms of the seventies and eighties. They brought us Gloria in *All in the Family*, Julie on *One Day at a Time*, Elyse in *Family Ties*, and Clair on the *Cosby Show*. And somehow each one of their pregnancy experiences seems incredibly similar: calm wife, hysterical husband, mishap on the way to the hospital, pacing in the waiting room, screaming in the delivery room, beaming smiles at the moment of birth. The clichés run hard and deep in Tinseltown, but in many ways it did appear that popular culture was embracing the idea. Beyond the nerve-wracked nuclear family there were the first few unwed mothers (Carla on *Cheers*; Maddie on *Moonlighting*) and numerous after-school specials and teen-friendly films about unknowing adolescents getting "into trouble." Times and attitudes were absolutely changing.

But when Murphy Brown announced her pregnancy in 1992, it spawned a national controversy when she vowed to raise the child on her own. Many were appalled at her decision; others saw Murphy as a symbol of the times: a professional, self-sufficient woman fully capable of raising a child on her own.

If it took op-ed coverage in the national dailies to bring pregnancy to the fore, then in a strange way it worked. Beginning in the nineties it seemed that pregnancy was more popular than ever. Perhaps it was Demi Moore's notorious *Vanity Fair* cover in 1991 that started a trend, but by the mid-nineties it seemed that everyone was having children: Cindy, Elle, Paulina, Stephanie, and Jada, all of whom stepped out and bravely bared their bodies, bulging belly buttons, swollen breasts, and all.

Pregnancy, apparently, became sexy and beautiful overnight. From television personalities Katie Couric to Phoebe on *Friends,* women's pregnancies were being written into storylines and shown in their entirety in front of national audiences. At the same time, stars who were pregnant but whose television characters weren't were artfully disguised during filming with inventive camera angles and discreetly placed props. Both Julia Louis-Dreyfus, who played Elaine on *Seinfeld*, and Sarah Jessica Parker, who played Carrie on *Sex and the City*, are two examples of popular nineties television actresses who carefully camouflaged their on-air pregnancies without having to write their weight gain into the script.

Today, our acceptance of pregnancy has come so far that reality television includes on-air births. It's not uncommon anymore to see real women in real hospitals grunting away and pushing a baby out. Our culture has become so interested in analyzing how other people live that shows like the Learning Channel's *A Baby Story* follow the development of babies, in intimate detail, from the first missed period to birth and beyond. That's a far cry from the days of Lucy, when she could only tell Ricky she was pregnant (or "having a baby") by incorporating the news into his nightclub act. Today, the media fully embraces pregnancy, as well they should. I love to see women flaunting their pregnancies on-screen, on the red carpet, and in everyday life. Why not revel in it? Every woman should.

MURPHY BROWN, 1992

CHEERS, 1983

THE NEWHART SHOW, 1989

THE COSBY SHOW, 1988

HOLLY ROCK-A-BYE BABY, 1993

FRIENDS, 1998

FATHER OF THE BRIDE, PART 2, 1995

MAD ABOUT YOU, 1998

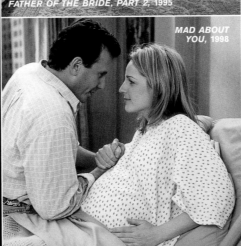

NINE MONTHS, 1995

THE PINK
CONDITION

ion editor Ellin Saltzman
ices what Liz Karlson,
rnity clothes editor and voice
erience, preaches,
is the time to look prettier
ever," they agree.
re-baby clothes need to be
y black or subdued colors
no more. Pretty pale shades
ot only becoming to
lexions, they set a young
heery mood."

FASHION ICON ELLIN SALTZMAN
IN *GLAMOUR*, 1961.

GLORIA STEINAM WITH
A PREGNANT JIMMY CARTER
ON THE COVER OF *MS.*, 1977

ALI McGRAW
PREGNANT WITH
SON JOSH, 1970.

ISABELLA ROSSELLINI
IN *VOGUE*, 1983.

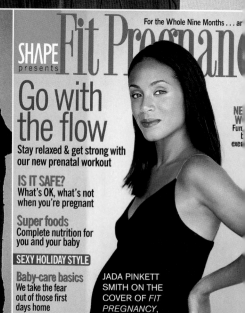

JADA PINKETT
SMITH ON THE
COVER OF *FIT
PREGNANCY*,
JANUARY 2001.

LEFT TO RIGHT: TOP: FRANK HURWIT/COURTESY OF GLAMOUR. CONDÉNAST PUBLICATIONS. MS: BETTMANN/CORBIS: BOTTOM: MICHAEL A. MCCARO/PDL. INC. DENIS PIEL/©VOGUE. CONDÉ NAST PUBLICATIONS. ©DEC/JAN 2001WEIDER PUBLICATIONS INC. REPRINTED WITH PERMISSION

"*LOVE STORY* OPENED AT THE END OF MY PREGNANCY AND I HAD TO DO AN ENORMOUS AMOUNT OF PUBLICITY, LOOKING DIFFERENT FOR EACH EVENT. I HAD BEEN WEARING A LOT OF HALSTON CLOTHES AT THE TIME, AND HE HAD TWO ARTISTS DOING INCREDIBLE TIE-DYE VELVET FOR HIM. I BOUGHT YARDS OF THE FABRIC AND HOLLY HARP, A BIG L.A. DESIGNER AT THE TIME, MADE ME SOME BEAUTIFUL EMPIRE DRESSES (WORN WITH BOOTS) FOR THE BIG NIGHTS. THE SINGLE OUTFIT I REMEMBER WEARING ALL THE TIME WAS MY FAVORITE: LONG BLACK JERSEY SKIRT, WHICH I HAD BOUGHT FROM HALSTON BEFORE I WAS PREGNANT. I WORE IT ALL THE TIME WITH A LONG, SKINNY, BODY-FITTING SWEATER. AFTER I GOT PREGNANT I CONTINUED TO WEAR IT; I JUST STOPPED BUTTONING THE WAISTBAND AND USED SAFETY PINS (BIGGER AND BIGGER AND BIGGER ONES!) TO FASTEN IT HIGH UP UNDER MY BREASTS."

— ALI MCGRAW, ACTRESS

holidays and
special occasions

Celebrate. This is what holidays and special occasions are for, reasons to gather with family and friends to recognize life's big events. Be it weddings, graduations, Thanksgiving dinners, or brunches, special occasions are cause to commemorate the milestones and to appreciate those who make our lifetime landmarks possible.

These events are also typically a reason to dress up, and this is why they tend to cause pregnant women considerable amounts of grief. Among the many emails I receive every week, there are always a few that focus on outfits for special occasions, those situations when you'll see, and be seen, by a number of people. Or if not a large number of people, at least the important people, the ones who are often as excited to see you as they are apt to critique you. Oh, look how you've grown, your Aunt Esther might say, squeezing your cheeks and patting your behind. This comment alone, not to mention her knowing smile, is reason enough to make you think twice about what you'll wear.

The goal is to get through these open-viewing occasions with the greatest of ease—and panache. With a little forethought, and some strategic considerations for color and cut, we can make sure that as disappointing as it may be for her, Aunt Esther has nothing more to say than, "Honey, don't you look great."

Weddings rank up there at the apogee of special events. Whether you're the bride, an attendant, or simply a guest, the aura of a wedding is inescapable. The celebration of love, commitment, and all the fairy tale accoutrements are steeped in age-old tradition. No matter how casual or intimate a ceremony might be, it still can make almost any woman sigh. And overwhelm almost any pregnant woman with stress.

Let's face it, you want to look good. No, great. If you're the bride, and we'll get to that in a moment, the above goes without saying; if you're not the bride, you have the drop-dead gorgeous image of her beauty to contend with. You may say that a good friend would never compare herself to the bride, but let's be honest for a second and admit that when you're eight months pregnant, the contrast between her figure and yours smarts just a bit.

Get over it. You may still remember how great it felt to slip into your own wedding dress, but pack that memory away for the moment and realize that today is not the day to be the belle of the ball. Today is the day to look lovely, and appropriate, and to remind yourself of the belief that a pregnant woman's presence at a wedding is a good-luck charm, which is a wonderful honor.

hair
CLEAN, SLEEK, AND SOPHIS-TICATED. LET THE FOCUS FALL ON YOUR FRESH FACE AND GLOWING SKIN.

jewlery
A SIMPLE STRAND OF PEARLS ALWAYS SETS AN ELEGANT TONE.

jacket
A DRESS COAT IS CHIC AND PROVIDES ESSENTIAL COV-ERAGE FOR ARMS AND HIPS.

purse
A SMALL, SIMPLE BAG IN A COMPLEMENTARY COLOR WILL PROVIDE ENOUGH ROOM FOR POWDER AND LIPSTICK.

fabric
SILK SHANTUNG HAS A LIT-TLE TEXTURE AND WEIGHT. IT'S NOT TOO CLINGY AND PROVIDES STRUCTURE WITHOUT BEING BOXY.

hemline
KEEP THE LENGTH A LITTLE ABOVE THE KNEE TO SHOW OFF YOUR LEGS AND MAIN-TAIN AN EVEN PROPORTION.

stockings
GO BARE. UNLESS THE TEMPERATURE IS BELOW ZERO, YOU CAN GET AWAY WITH NAKED LEGS FOR ONE NIGHT.

shoes
OPEN-TOES SHOW OFF A LOT OF SKIN. THIS HEEL IS HIGH ENOUGH TO BE SEXY YET STILL COMFORTABLE.

MICHAEL MYERS

guests

As a guest you have a wide range of options, and these will vary depending on whether it's a garden, daytime, or evening affair. One suggestion: when deciding how dressy to go, consider your relationship with the couple. If the bride's your best friend or a member of the family, pull out the stops; if she's a good acquaintance or office mate, play it a little more low key.

day
THIS FLOUNCY DRESS WITH ITS SWEET CAP SLEEVES IS FEMININE BUT NOT TOO DEMURE. PERFECT FOR AN AFTERNOON OR OUTDOOR AFFAIR.

night
EVENING EVENTS ARE OFTEN BLACK TIE. TRY A DRAMATIC LONG SKIRT AND STRAPLESS TOP. THIS FLOOR-LENGTH WRAP IS A SPECTACULAR ACCENT.

"A SLIGHT HEEL IS THE PERFECT LOOK WHEN YOU ARE PREGNANT. IT IS EASY TO WALK IN AND ALSO MORE SLIMMING THAN FLATS."

**— AERIN LAUDER,
VICE PRESIDENT OF WORLD MARKETING, ESTÉE LAUDER**

fall

A LONG-LINED PANT SUIT IN AN AUTUMNAL COLOR IS SMART AND STYLISH WHEN PUMPED UP WITH THE RIGHT ACCESSORIES.

spring

FOR MORE FORMAL OCCASIONS, SEQUINS OR PAILLETTES CAN BE VERY GLAMOROUS. USE SPARINGLY AND STAY WITH A SOFT, SINGLE-TONED PALETTE.

Brides and Guests: Down the Aisle in Style

TOP ROW: DESIGNER VERA WANG, JERRY HALL, SOCIALITE JENNIFER CREEL, IMAN, ALEXANDRA VON FURSTENBERG. BOTTOM ROW: AERIN LAUDER, MODEL CAROL ALT, PRINCESS CAROLINE OF MONACO, DIANA, PRINCESS OF WALES.

here comes the bride

There once was a time when all brides wore white. There once was also a time when all brides were virgins, though if you're reading this and you're pregnant and engaged, you've clearly debunked that rule. So as far as I'm concerned, all bets are off when it comes to traditional white. If you are a pregnant bride, you don't have to wear it unless you want to, and by all means you certainly don't have to wear a conventional dress.

Today, many brides, pregnant or not, allow themselves to step outside of the box. Pastels, or even jewel tones for a winter wedding, are a beautiful antidote to white or ivory. Shapes are simple, clean, and elegant, such as slip dresses, A-lines, simple suits, and strapless columns. All are lovely options and great alternatives to the huge tulle skirts and wedding-cake dresses that will only make you look awkward and far bigger than you are.

The good news is a taseful, elegant dress is quite easy to find. You could visit a personal dressmaker or tailor, but most pregnancy boutiques that do evening wear can usually adapt a style and fabric for a wedding dress. The only question, then, is style. Here are some suggestions that will help you stand out on your special day.

OOH LA LA! MODEL KRISTEN MCMENEMY AND HER HUSBAND MILES AT THEIR 1997 LONDON WEDDING.

4 weddings (and a baby)

traditional
FOR THE ARCHETYPAL BRIDE, I PREFER A LONG, LEAN, COLUMNAR LOOK. THE UNCOMPLICATED LINES OF THIS DRESS ARE BEAUTIFUL, AND THE EMPIRE WAIST ACCENTUATES YOUR NECK AND SHOULDERS. ABSOLUTELY PICTURE PERFECT.

informal
THE SIMPLE, STRAIGHT LINE OF THIS LINEN SHEATH IS TIMELESS. I LOVE THE WHISPER OF COLOR AND THE GRACEFUL EFFECT OF A DELICATE WRAP. JUST ENOUGH WHITE TO MAKE YOU FEEL LIKE A BRIDE.

"IF YOU OBEY ALL THE RULES, YOU MISS ALL THE FUN." – **KATHARINE HEPBURN**

beach
A DIAPHANOUS WRAP DRESS IS BREEZY AND CAREFREE. SPAGHETTI STRAPS AND A DEEP V NECKLINE ARE SEXY AND REFINED, BUT I CAN STILL SEE THIS DRESS WITH BARE FEET.

daytime
A CLASSIC DAYTIME SUIT IS AN ELEGANT CHOICE FOR A SMALL, INTIMATE GATHERING OR SECOND WEDDING. SELECT AN UNDERSTATED, FLATTERING COLOR AND HIGHLIGHT WITH DRESSIER ACCESSORIES.

Question: My wedding is in May and I'll be six months pregnant at the time. I have my heart set on a vintage dress. Is this possible?
—Wendy, San Diego, CA

Answer: Vintage can be tricky. Your best bet is to look for a forties bias cut—think Greta Garbo in *Grand Hotel*—or a short empire cut in a bold color. If it's a traditional look you're after, that will be perfect. What a statement!

CROSS YOUR HEART: MODEL
PEGGY MOFFITT FINDS HER
INSPIRATION IN A SEVENTIES
STYLE BY RUDY GERNREICH.

rehearsal dinners

Less formal than the wedding itself, rehearsal dinners are typically comfortable, casual affairs, sometimes even with special themes such as barbecues, barn dances, Mexican fiestas, or island luaus. And although these special themes make for whimsical attire, luckily no one expects you to look like a rodeo queen if you're pregnant.

luau
HEAD FOR THE ISLANDS IN THIS FUN PRINT DRESS. THE HALTER TOP SHOWS OFF YOUR ARMS AND SHOULDERS WHILE OFFERING YOU ADJUSTABLE SUPPORT.

barbecues
AN ALL-AMERICAN COMBINATION: A CLASSIC BUTTON-DOWN IN RED AND WHITE CHECKS WITH SLIM WHITE PANTS. CHUNKY TURQUOISE JEWELRY IS A SPOT OF COLOR.

"IS FASHION IMPORTANT: WELL, MY DEAR—
YOU HAVE TO GET DRESSED." – **CARRIE DONOVAN,
FASHION LEGEND**

country club
A SIMPLE SUNDRESS AND LADYLIKE
CARDIGAN ARE PROPER FOR A MORE
FORMAL AFFAIR. HAVE A LITTLE FUN WITH
SUBTLE STRIPES IN SPRINGTIME COLORS.

beach party
THE GRAPHIC QUALITY OF THIS BOLD,
BLACK-AND-WHITE PRINT IS VERY MODERN.
THE TANK TOP IS SNUG AND HAS A BUILT-IN
BRA AND ADJUSTABLE STRAPS TO HOLD YOU IN.

attendants

Most brides are fairly generous when it comes to their pregnant attendants. In my experience, unless the company that makes the bridesmaids' dresses is willing to make a maternity dress (and this is rare), most brides are comfortable with letting a pregnant friend get by with wearing the same color. Most boutiques have color cards to match the pale pink she's selected, so as long as the bride doesn't choose a floral or tropical print, you should be okay.

Style-wise, go simple and let go of the idea that your silhouette needs to match those of the other attendants. And before you buy anything, ask the bride her opinion first. Hopefully, she'll be fine with whatever you choose. If she's not, you're probably off the hook altogether!

holiday gatherings

Many American families these days are spread out across the country so holidays become the only time to connect. That means that when you do get to see your relatives, it's time to savor. It's also time to spend a little extra effort planning what to wear. Even the most put-together woman needs something special for the holidays, so here are some outfit ideas appropriate for church, synagogue, and at-home get-togethers exuding good cheer.

Deck the Halls
ORSON WELLS TAKES TO THE
DANCE FLOOR WITH PREGNANT
WIFE RITA HAYWORTH.

rites of passage

These are the events you'll recall in photo albums and home videos, the events you'll look back on and talk about for years. These rites of passage are key mark-ers in our lives, and although right now you may be horrified at the idea of recording your pregnant figure for posterity, ten years from now you'll be glad you did.

baby and wedding showers
HAPPY OCCASIONS CALL FOR BURSTS OF COLOR. AVOID BLACK ALTOGETHER AND CHOOSE A SIMPLE RED SHIFT DRESS WITH A FLATTERING NECKLINE. A HOT PINK SWEATER IS A JOYOUS ADDITION.

graduations
LILAC IS LOVELY FOR A SPRINGTIME GRADUATION. HERE, THE DIPPED-IN-COLOR CONCEPT WORKS BEAUTIFULLY WITH A PRETTY PRINT DRESS AND MATCHING CARDIGAN.

What you wear, then, should be something that stands out but doesn't make you too self-conscious, something that will make you feel happy when the photos come back and you put them away to share with your future child in the years to come. What a joy it will be to see you looked so good.

christenings and brisses
RELIGIOUS EVENTS, ESPECIALLY THOSE IN CHURCH, REQUIRE SOMETHING SUBDUED AND GENTEEL. A CHARCOAL GRAY PENCIL SKIRT TOPPED WITH A PASTEL SWEATER SET COVERS YOUR SHOULDERS IN APPROPRIATE FASHION.

memorials and wakes
PAY YOUR RESPECTS WITH A SIMPLE AND ELEGANT BLACK DRESS. KEEP THE LENGTH BELOW THE KNEE AND ACCESSORIZE WITH PEARLS, WHICH MATCH THE PIPING AROUND THE COLLAR OF THIS SHEATH.

easter sunday
CELEBRATE THE HOLIDAY BY DIPPING YOURSELF IN EASTER EGG COLORS. COVER YOUR SHOULDERS IN CHURCH WITH A COTTON CARDIGAN, AND THEN REMOVE TO SHOW OFF THE SLIM LINES OF THIS GENTLY FITTED DRESS.

4th of july
CREATE SOME FIREWORKS OF YOUR OWN WITH A DEEP V-NECK TEE AND A SHORT SKIRT. USE THESE SUMMER DAYS TO SHOW OFF YOUR LEGS, AND TAKE THAT SKIRT AS HIGH AS YOU DARE.

"THERE WAS ONE ITEM THAT I COULD NOT HAVE GOTTEN THROUGH MY PREGNANCY WITHOUT—A COMFORTABLE, EASY DRESS THAT DIDN'T MAKE ME FEEL AS IF I WERE WEARING A TENT."
— MELISSA RIVERS, *E! ENTERTAINMENT*

labor day picnic

TOILE PRINT CAPRIS AND A SPORTY TANK ARE COOL AND
COMFORTABLE FOR A CASUAL, OUTDOOR AFFAIR. AGAIN,
THROW A COTTON CARDIGAN AROUND YOUR SHOULDERS
TO WARD OFF AN EVENING CHILL.

jewish holidays

A CONSERVATIVE SKIRT AND TRADITIONAL SWEATER SET
ARE FITTING FOR THE HIGH HOLIDAYS, ESPECIALLY IF
YOUR MORNING IS SPENT IN SYNAGOGUE.

maternity must have:
pencil skirt

1

A SOFT CASHMERE
IN CHEERFUL RED
IMMEDIATELY PUTS YOU
IN A HOLIDAY MOOD.

2 + 3

THE ESSENTIAL SWEATER
SET: A SLEEVELESS
TURTLENECK AND BLACK,
RIBBED CARDIGAN.

4

SLIM-FITTING,
SHOW-STOPPING
LACE PANTS
IN ELEGANT IVORY.

5

A KNEE-LENGTH
LEATHER SKIRT
IN SOPHISTICATED
WINTER WHITE.

6

CLASSIC HOUNDS-
TOOTH PANTS IN
GO-ANYWHERE
BLACK AND WHITE.

**1 + 6 =
thanksgiving**

**1 + 4 =
cocktail parties**

**2 + 3 + 5 =
sunday brunch**

m
mix
+
m
match

'tis the season

Beginning with Thanksgiving, the holiday season feels like a whirlwind of events and parties—and by the time New Year's rolls around, you often feel like a whirling dervish. This perpetual overdrive can be especially taxing when you're pregnant. Still, the excitement of the holidays is also irrisistible, what with turkeys roasting and cookies baking, snowflakes, candles in the window, and Christmas carols. The clothes we choose should celebrate this festive time. And although you're apt to run into the same people again and again around the punch bowl, even non-pregnant people tend to expect a lot of mileage from their holiday gear, and as I've mentioned before, it would take an extremely indelicate person to point out a repeated outfit on a pregnant woman.

1 + 5 =
christmas dinner

2 + 4 =
new year's eve

2 + 3 + 6 =
new year's day

third trimester

pre-pregnancy
you

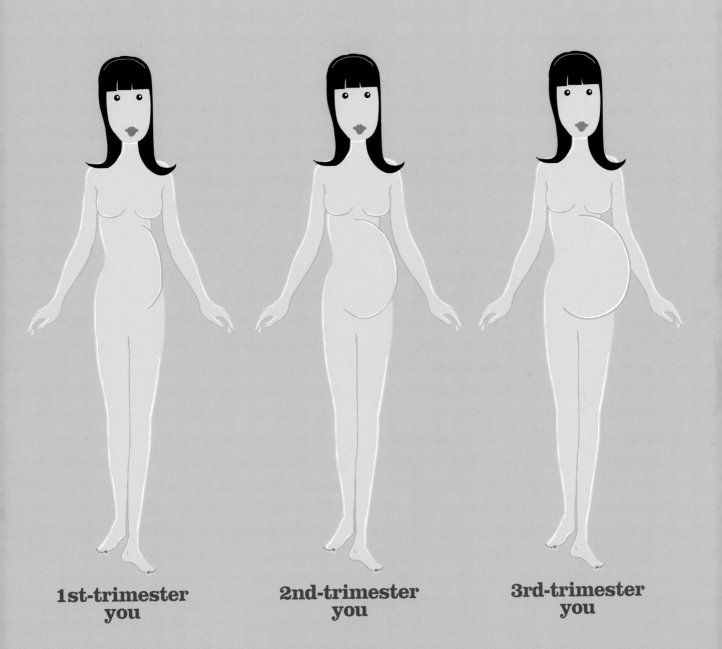

1st-trimester you

2nd-trimester you

3rd-trimester you

This is it. The homestretch. The moment you've been waiting for with excitement or anxiety, or most likely a mix of the two, is just around the corner. For months now this "giving birth thing" has seemed like an impossibility, but with your belly now reaching mind-bending proportions, it seems pretty clear this is really going to happen. And soon. Ask any woman who's been pregnant and we all agree: the last few weeks can be torture. You're too big to move, too full to eat, too nervous to sleep. You're over being pregnant, you want to meet your baby, and you want your body back.

The first time around, every woman thinks that she's going to go early. With a month to go you start counting the days and assessing every pain and twitch. Is this labor? you ask. Probably not. As Dr. Schiller says, the majority of babies come pretty close to your due date. And as your due date nears, every bone in your aching body gets in bed each night saying "this is it." You've packed a bag, including snacks and pillows, and you close your eyes with the thought that tomorrow you'll be a mom. Then the morning comes, and you're still pregnant! Today's technology may allow us to determine the exact day, if not the hour, that we conceived, but all of that means diddly when you're overdue. At the stage all the nesting in the world won't do much to ease your state of mind.

So what does all this last-minute "agita" mean for your wardrobe? It means that as your due date approaches—and passes!— it's all about comfort. During those last few weeks, when you're really big and moving as slowly as a snail, give yourself full permission to wear whatever you want. If this means an oversized sweatshirt, a muumuu, or a 1950s housedress, go for it. Go for whatever makes you feel comfortable, because the truth of the matter is, you're probably not feeling so attractive at this point, so there's no need to sweat the stylish details. If you can actually get up in the morning, blow-dry your hair, and put on some makeup, you're doing extremely well.

Up until this eleventh hour, however, you should be absolutely fine. If you shopped smartly during your second trimester, the wardrobe you purchased should allow you to segue right into your third trimester. Yes, your tummy really will get bigger than you ever imagined, but unless you have *nothing* that fits anymore, you shouldn't be buying anything new at this stage. In fact, save those final few weeks, the third trimester is when many of the clothes you bought really look good. Maternity clothes actually fit best during your seventh and eighth months because you can now, as they say, finally "fill them out." No more rolled-down waistbands. You're big and wonderful. Suffice it to say, that pillow you shoved in your belly three months ago is now serving you very well.

For many women, their third trimester is when they feel, and look, their best. People smile at you and stop you on the street to ask when you're due and what you're having. Even if your feet are swollen and your sciatica is acting up, there's something truly amazing about what is going on inside you. Beauty on the inside does translate to beauty on the outside, and your state of mind paired with the body-conscious fashions you selected will now be announcing that.

Because you've come a long way. Believe it or not, by the end of your pregnancy your baby is approximately 20 inches long and probably weighs between 6 and 9 pounds. In 40 weeks, the pea-sized heartbeat you saw on your first sonogram has turned into a living, breathing baby. Take a moment to congratulate yourself. Dismiss your worries about weight gain and try to quell your fears of labor and delivery. Because, believe me, when you'll soon be holding your newborn in your arms, nothing else much matters.

travel

Pregnant or not, women always shop before they travel. It must be some biological imperative, the notion that we must buy a new sweater, new skirt, and of course new lingerie before we go on a big trip. Unless you're planning a backpacking trek through the jungles of Thailand (which seems unlikely if you're seven months pregnant) you'll probably agree that the idea of a specially planned and purchased pregnancy travel wardrobe is, if nothing else, a guilty pleasure. After wrestling indigestion, leg cramps, and varicose veins, it's not hard to convince yourself that you absolutely need a few new items for that last before-the-baby vacation.

So take a moment to entertain what they're wearing in Paris this spring, even if, like most people, you travel for business, to visit family, or to attend your nephew's bar mitzvah in Detroit. Travel, in this context, can be trying: getting to the airport, braving the lines, the security, suffering hours of re-circulated air on the plane, and in the end, arriving in a new city with a different time zone and unfamiliar climate. Having that "must have" item of the season neatly packed in your bag can definitely help you endure these inconveniences.

But travel can also be a much-needed escape. Why not find a small window of time when you can travel solely for pleasure. If not now, then when? I tell many of my clients, especially those expecting their first child, to try to squeeze in one more vacation alone with their partner. I'm sure I'm not the first one to say this, but months from now when you're sleep deprived and mopping up spit, you'll be extremely happy that you got away.

DEPARTURES

Gate	Los Angeles
Gate	New York
Gate 1	Paris
Gate	Chicago
Gate 2	Denver
Gate 25	NOW BOARDING

planning your trip

A vacation is sort of a microcosm. It's a snapshot of time, and fashion-wise almost a condensed version of all the considerations you've had throughout your nine months. You'll want to bring a few, and I repeat, a *few,* items that can adapt to several situations. Many women make the mistake of packing far too much. You want to be prepared, you say, for any situation; but the truth is, unless it's already on your itinerary you're probably not getting invited to any royal balls at the last minute. Nor will you find yourself needing a bathing suit in Prague (What if there's a pool at the hotel?) or a leather jacket in the Bahamas (Doesn't it get cold at night?).

Thankfully we live in a world where any number of web sites can provide you with a week's worth of highs and lows for almost any city across the globe. Determining the weather in your destination makes your packing job much simpler. Sure, things come up, and I'm not telling you to be completely unprepared for the surprise cold snap or heat wave, but before you pack lay everything out on your bed and really try to think about what you'll be doing on your trip. This makes it so much easier to visualize what you will actually wear.

the business trip

Everything that applies to dressing for pregnancy is twice as essential when you're traveling for business and you want to be neat, clean, and wrinkle free. "Minimal" is definitely the watchword, and the idea that you need a new outfit for every meeting is just preposterous. When traveling for business, pack seasonless items in dark colors and transitional fabrics that travel well. Layering is the answer here, especially if you're flying from coast to coast.

When I was pregnant, I found that matte jersey was my best solution for travel. I was commuting between New York and L.A. a lot, working on my new Beverly Hills store, and I needed clothes that were suitable for casual, professional, and even dressy occasions. Matte jersey was the answer. It rolled up into nothing in my bag, making packing a breeze for such a short trip, and best of all I could get away without checking my bag. Matte jersey is also incredibly versatile and adapts well from sight-seeing to business meetings to nice restaurants at night.

IF YOUR WORK ALLOWS YOU TO BE MORE CASUAL, A RELAXED WRAP SWEATER IS IDEAL FOR THE PLANE. IT'S SOFT AND COZY AND CAN SIMPLY BE REMOVED TO REVEAL A SHIRT UNDERNEATH IF YOU'RE TRAVELING TO A WARMER CLIMATE.

CLASSIC TWIN SETS WON'T WRINKLE LIKE A
JACKET AND YET ACHIEVE THE SAME CLEAN AND
PULLED-TOGETHER LOOK. RED PANTS ALSO
LOOK NEAT AND PROFESSIONAL, BUT FUN, TOO.

WHEN TRAVELING TO COLDER CLIMES, TRY TRIM BROWN PANTS
WITH A SWEATER IN A MATCHING TONE. COMPLETE THE OUTFIT
WITH LOAFERS—THEY SLIDE OFF AND ON EASILY, AND UNLIKE
HEELS DON'T CONTRIBUTE TO THE HIGH-ALTITUDE SWELLING.

in the air

When you're pregnant, the idea of spending several hours in a small, narrow, barely reclining seat can feel like torture. Add the dehydrated air and distasteful food and it's truly a miracle that pregnant women ever fly. Comfort, obviously, is of prime importance when deciding what to wear on a plane. You want something non-restricting, breathable, and soft. You want something that will keep you warm when the air-conditioning is set too high (isn't it always?), and you want something that can take you to your hotel or, if necessary, translate to business attire. Opposite, some thoughts on translating your in-air outfit to life on the ground.

on the ground

+ = Pack away your comfy cardigan and remove a cleanly pressed jacket from your hanging bag.

+ = Exchange your loafers for a more professional shoe. Stack heels will do the trick.

+ = Turn up the volume with strategic jewelry, particularly if you're headed to an evening event.

"EVERY TIME WE FLEW, I WORE MY MATTE JERSEY PANTS AND A CARDIGAN SWEATER. THE OUTFIT WAS COMFORTABLE AND IT LOOKED REALLY PUT TOGETHER: LIGHTWEIGHT AND LOOSE FITTING ON THE BODY WITHOUT LOOKING SLOPPY."
— CHYNNA PHILLIPS, SINGER

LEFT TO RIGHT—TOP: BETTMANN/CORBIS; NEAL PETERS COLLECTION - HULTON ARCHIVE BY GETTY IMAGES. BOTTOM: DAVID HURN/MAGNUM PHOTOS; GLOBE PHOTOS; BETTMANN/CORBIS

Around the World . . . in 40 Weeks

TOP ROW: JACQUELINE AND JOHN F. KENNEDY WITH CAROLINE; BARBRA STREISAND; PRINCESS DIANA AND PRINCE CHARLES OF WALES; BOTTOM ROW: JANE FONDA IN ST. TROPEZ, PRINCESS GRACE OF MONACO IN LONDON, SINGER ARLO GUTHRIE AND WIFE JACKIE IN LONDON.

weekend get-aways

Go someplace you've never gone before. New York. New Orleans. London. San Francisco. Find a city that appeals to you and a hotel you can afford and spend a couple of days living the high life. I love exploring a new city—the charming restaurants, quaint back streets, quirky stores that you wouldn't find anyplace else. It's so exciting to immerse yourself in a new place, and you'll be very glad you packed one smashing outfit for a night at the theater and a dinner-for-two after.

SPLURGE!

SAVE!   **SAVE!**

SPLURGE!

SAVE!   **SAVE!**

SILK IS A LUXURY. IT FEELS FABULOUS NEXT TO YOUR SKIN AND INSTANTLY MAKES ANY OUTFIT DRESSY ENOUGH FOR NIGHT. CHOOSE A CITY-SLEEK PATTERN OR COLOR AND PAIR WITH SIMPLE BLACK PANTS OR A SLITTED SKIRT.

YVES SAINT LAURENT INTRODUCED THE TUXEDO PANT FOR WOMEN AND NOW IT RANKS UP THERE WITH THE CHICEST ITEMS IN ANY FASHION-CONSCIOUS CLOSET. A WHITE SHELL OR BLACK V-NECK SWEATER IS A PERFECT COMPLEMENT.

Accessories

**Easy-to-pack items.
Inexpensive, fun jewelry:
Bangles. Chunky rings.
Anything that adds a dash of color.
Sunglasses. A sun hat. Sunscreen.
Comfortable shoes for walking.
Boots if it's cold.
A good, roomy bag for day trips.
Extra water
and snacks for a long flight.**

Madonna with Child
THE PERENNIALLY FASHIONABLE MADONNA LOOKED AMAZING DURING BOTH OF HER PREGNANCIES. NEVER ONE TO SHY AWAY FROM EXPOSING HERSELF, SHE LET HER BELLY SHOW WITH PRIDE—ON THE STREET AND BY THE SHORE. WAY TO GO!

maternity must have: man-style shirt

"ONE OF MY FAVORITES DURING PREGNANCY WAS A CLASSIC WHITE BUTTON-DOWN SHIRT. THAT AND A PAIR OF SUNGLASSES AND YOU ALWAYS LOOK GOOD!" — KELLY PRESTON, ACTRESS

KIMORA LEE SIMMONS, HERE, WITH HUSBAND RUSSELL SIMMONS, SHOWS US HOW SWELL A SARONG CAN LOOK.

ACTOR MARK RUFFALO CAN'T GET ENOUGH OF HIS WIFE, SANDRA, IN HER SEXY WRAP DRESS.

traveling for pleasure

Do it now, baby. Pleasure takes on a whole new meaning once a child is in the picture and three hours of uninterrupted sleep is a blessed event. At the moment you can't imagine catching any less than eight hours of shut-eye, but soon that will change. So indulge yourself. Revel in sleeping late, breakfast in bed, and lounging in a (not-too-hot) tub. Enjoy shopping, romantic dinners, and walks along the beach. Whether you jet off to an island, take a quiet weekend at a bed and breakfast, or simply check into a hotel for the night, the most important thing about your last pre-childbirth trip, or babymoon as I call it, is spending uninterrupted time with your partner. Then get ready to welcome the newest addition to your lives.

1

THE CLASSIC
WHITE TEE TAKES
YOU ANYWHERE.
3/4 SLEEVES
ALSO GUARD
AGAINST THE SUN.

2

A BASIC BLACK
TANK IS BOTH
SUPPORTIVE
AND SLIMMING.
IF YOU BRING ONE
SUIT, THIS IS IT.

3

IN A STRIKING
COLOR, THE
PEASANT TUNIC
IS FUN AND
FESTIVE. THE PER-
FECT COVER-UP.

4

WHITE DRAW-
STRING PANTS
ARE AN ISLAND
STAPLE. COOL,
CRISP, AND OH-SO-
COMFORTABLE.

5

A *PAREO* IN A
BOLD PRINT ADDS
COLOR TO YOUR
POOLSIDE ATTIRE.
DON'T LEAVE
HOME WITHOUT IT.

6

FOR BOTH
ROMANTIC
DINNERS AND
POOLSIDE
COCKTAILS, A
SUNDRESS IS IT.

**1 + 5 =
light lunch**

**1 + 4 =
shopping**

**2 + 5 =
poolside**

**6 =
dressy dinner**

south of the border

When the winter winds blow and the sky seems a perpetual shade of gray, I suggest heading south for some warm weather relief. Ski vacations are difficult when you're pregnant, so why not opt instead for a little lounging on the beach? Plus, warm-weather trips are a snap to pack for. All you need are a couple of sundresses, a cardigan, a *pareo,* one bathing suit (it will dry overnight), and a pair of slides. You'll want a sun hat and a cover-up for your shoulders, too, but honestly, that should be it. Resist the urge to pack formal wear for evenings on the veranda. These days, few resorts are very dressy and the joy of the beach is to strip down to next to nothing.

**2 + 3 =
sun screen**

**2 + 4 =
beach stroll**

**3 + 4 =
casual dinner**

WARM SUN, COOL BREEZE:
PRINCESS STEPHANIE OF MONACO
RELAXES BY THE POOL IN
MONTE CARLO.

Q+A

Question: My husband just came home with tickets to Hawaii! I'm six months pregnant, it's January, and the idea of a bathing suit terrifies me. All of the bikinis in my closet are way too small. What can I do to cover myself up?

— Anna, Chicago, IL

Answer: First things first: There's a big difference between being overweight and being pregnant, and at six months there's probably little doubt that you're expecting. Most people, I'm sure your husband included, find a pregnant woman's figure very sexy. Especially her belly. As far as buying a suit, swim wear is now available year round. Look for a supportive tankini. It provides more coverage than a typical bikini and can also be rolled up while you're sunning. Just don't forget the sunblock.

beauty

Pregnancy can wreak havoc on your beauty regimen. Over the course of 40 weeks your body undergoes so many incredible changes, not the least of which is a hormonal field day on your hair and face. For some fortunate women, the transformation can be great: thick hair, glowing skin, resilient nails. For others, however, pregnancy is like an undersea creature, dormant since adolescence and now resurfacing for a gulp of air.

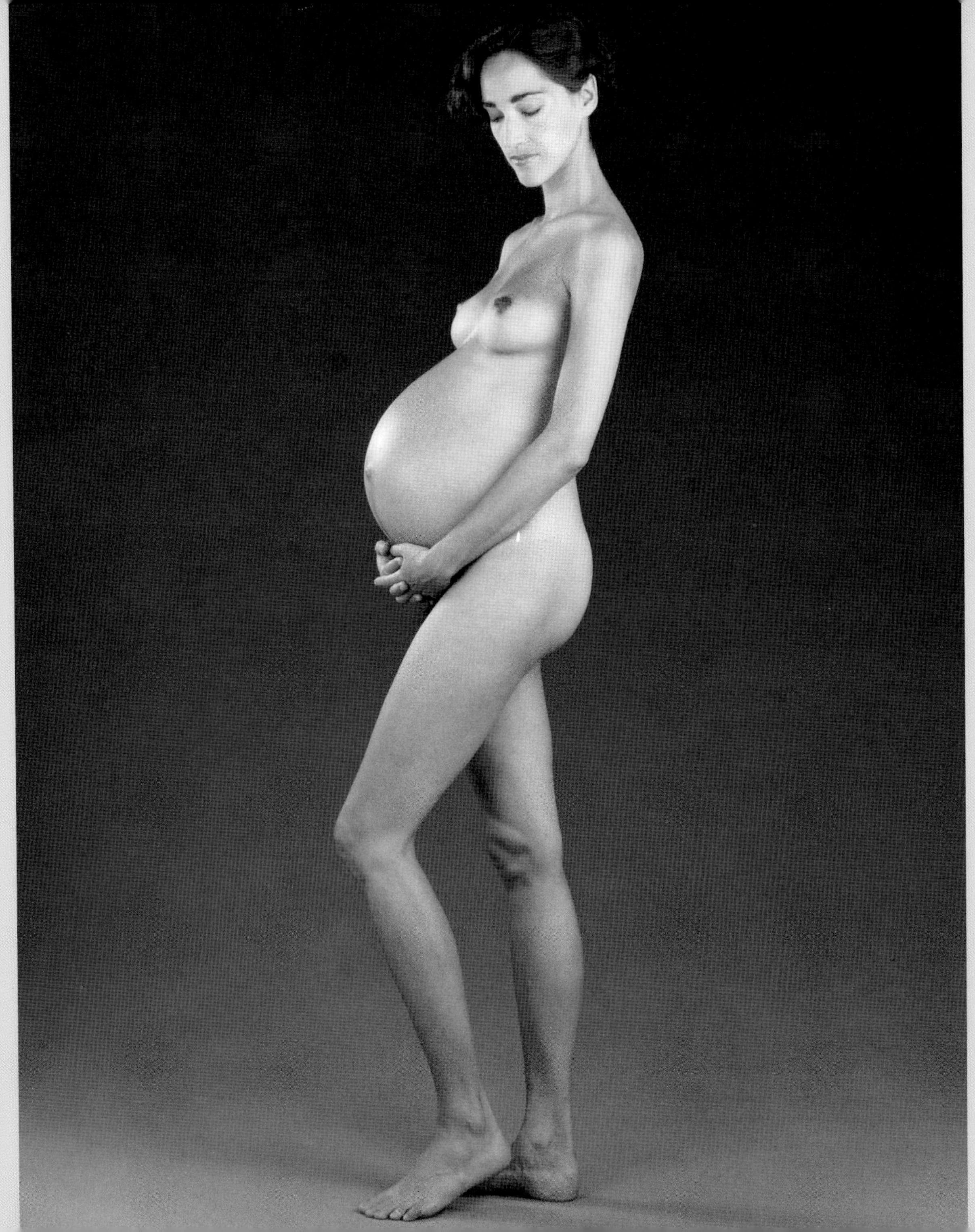

Skincare

Every woman is unique. No two women carry the same or gain the same amount of weight. You've heard this countless times from your obstetrician or midwife, right? And when it comes to your skin, this statement is equally tue.

"Everyone reacts to pregnancy differently," says Trish McEvoy, makeup artist and owner of Trish McEvoy. Some women's skin improves during pregnancy; some breaks out. Finding a concrete answer to such a difficult predicament can be hard, and Trish strongly suggests seeing a dermatologist, especially if you're breaking out. Find someone you trust and who can work hand-in-glove with your OB or midwife. Most important, find someone who can advise you on what you can use—and what you can't. This will vary from doctor to doctor. I know many women who avoid prescription products altogether when they're pregnant, including acne-fighting topicals and wrinkle-busting creams. This may seem extreme, but your doctor will be able to advise you, and the truth is the remedies for pregnancy-related issues are pretty limited.

If you are breaking out a lot and you are restricted in your medical options, Trish suggests regular facials. They can be incredibly cleansing and, better still, relaxing. It's always a treat to take an hour at a spa, but just be sure to let the technician know that you're pregnant so they can adjust your treatment accordingly.

And then there are women who don't break out but who become unbearably itchy and dry, feeling like their skin—head to toe, and especially the belly—is as parched as the Sahara. If that scaly status is your lot, daily moisturizing is an absolute necessity. Slather on the cocoa butter or essential oil or the belly balm your best friend bought you. Enjoy the luxurious feel of super-soft skin; just don't mistake these ministrations as an antidote to stretch marks. The fact is that those of us who are hereditarily doomed to get stretch marks will, and those of us who aren't, well, you might want to keep that to yourself.

One thing Trish does recommend for all pregnant women is sunscreen. Your skin becomes more sensitive to the sun when you're pregnant, so it's important to use a strong sunblock daily. Whether you're pregnant or not, try something like titanium dioxide, which doesn't contain any chemicals. It will also help prevent dark pigmentation patches, or the pregnancy mask, that affects some women.

Beyond that, Trish says, strive to be as natural as possible in your beauty routine. Use a lightweight moisturizer, wash your face with tepid (not hot or cold) water, and use a gentle cleanser or wash. Use a light lip balm or gloss. Keep your colors neutral and stick with makeup that doesn't require a lot of thought. Many woman have a natural glow anyway when they're pregnant. There's no need to add new products or rituals. Keep it simple.

Haircare

A brief note on hair: everyone's hair grows during pregnancy. It gets thicker thanks to the army of hormones marching through your body, and for the course of your pregnancy you should be blessed with some of the lushest and most beautiful hair of your adult life. Enjoy it. Find a style that suits you (I always think longer hair makes your face look thinner when you're pregnant) and check in with your doctor before you use color or highlights as practitioners feel differently on this issue.

Then steel yourself. Although it doesn't happen to all women, some new mothers do experience postpartum hair loss. Strands on the pillow, in your hairbrush, braided through your fingers after a bath. There is nothing we can do to prevent postpartum hair loss, but in fact you shouldn't end up with less hair than you started with—it's just that that extra hair won't stick around. It's a hormonal thing, as is everything else when you're pregnant. The up side is that you can color your hair to your heart's content. So pick a fun new shade and style—that should do the trick.

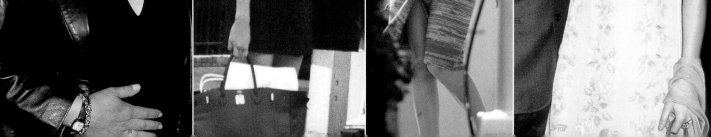

"THINGS CAN GET OVERWHELMING WHEN YOU'RE PREGNANT AND IT'S EASY TO STOP PAMPERING YOURSELF. BUT NOW MORE THAN EVER IS THE TIME FOR YOU TO TAKE CARE OF YOURSELF. TAKE A FEW MINUTES TO APPLY SOME MAKEUP; IT DOES A LOT TO BOOST YOUR MOOD. QUICK AND EASY WAYS TO MAKE A DIFFERENCE: BLEND CREAMY CONCEALER ON UNDER-EYE CIRCLES TO LOOK LIKE YOU'VE HAD A FULL NIGHT'S REST (WHEN YOU'VE REALLY ONLY HAD A FEW HOURS OF SLEEP); USE A LITTLE FOUNDATION AROUND YOUR NOSE AND CHIN, OR WHEREVER YOU NEED TO EVEN OUT YOUR SKIN TONE; AND SWEEP A PRETTY SHADE OF BLUSH ON THE APPLES OF YOUR CHEEKS FOR A HEALTHY NATURAL-LOOKING GLOW."
— BOBBI BROWN, FOUNDER AND CEO OF BOBBI BROWN COSMETICS

Model Behavior

THE WORLD'S MOST PHOTOGRAPHED WOMEN STRUT THEIR PREGNANCIES IN STYLE. TOP ROW: VENDELA AND FREDERIQUE, AMBER VALETTA, CHRISTIE BRINKLEY AND HUSBAND PETER COOK, ELLE MACPHERSON, ANNETTE ROCHE AND HUSBAND MATT LAUER. BOTTOM ROW: EMME, YASMIN, LAETITIA CASTA, HELENA CHRISTIANSEN.

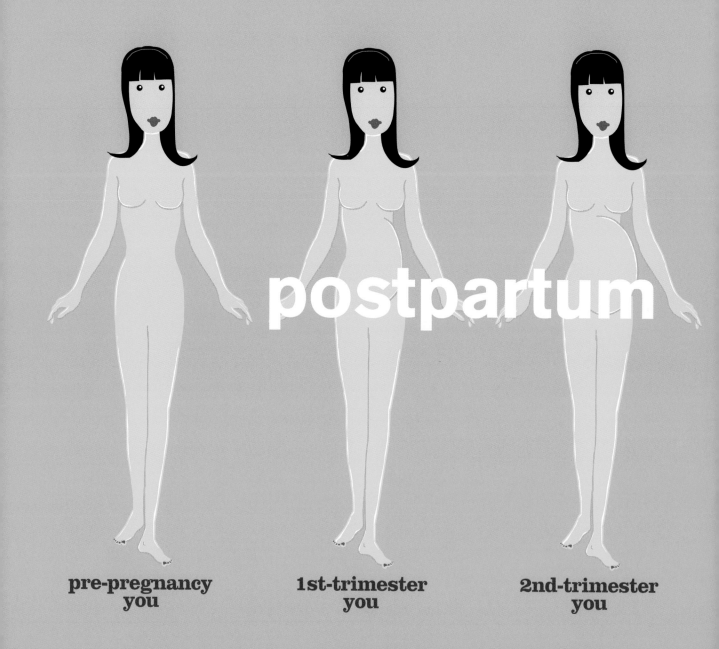

**pre-pregnancy
you**

**1st-trimester
you**

**2nd-trimester
you**

postpartum

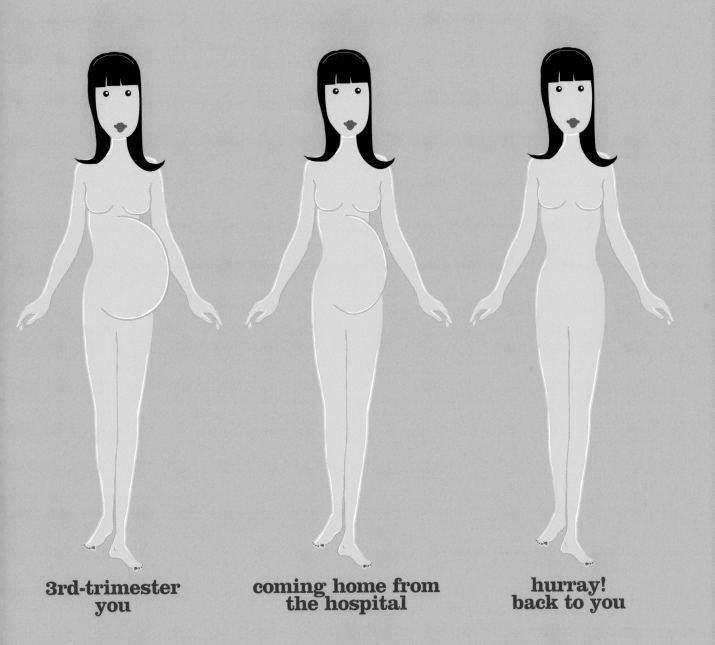

**3rd-trimester
you**

**coming home from
the hospital**

**hurray!
back to you**

So here you are: a mother. It's everything and nothing you imagined. You're exhausted, overwhelmed, and sleep-deprived. You're ecstatic, elated, and blissfully in love with your new baby. Confusing? Yes. Your first few postpartum weeks are a heady time and wrestling with what to wear can be hard when you're dying to fit back into your old clothes but can't. So don't believe anyone who tells you that you'll be back into your regular clothes in no time. It just doesn't happen. Even if you breastfeed and if you gained only a scant twenty-five pounds. After giving birth, everyone has extra weight (and extra skin!) to contend with, so although you're longing to stow your pregnancy clothes in the basement—or set them on fire if you think you're done with the baby thing—try to resist the urge to give them all away.

First of all, you'll need something comfortable to wear home from the hospital and to get you through those first few weeks at home. Feel free to jettison the giant pants you wore during your final month, but be generous to yourself and hold on to your early second trimester and transitional items for just a little while. Overall, I recommend that your postpartum wardrobe incorporate as many of these transitional clothes as possible. Just as you traded up while you were newly pregnant, now is the time to trade down. Those pants you bought that were a few sizes too big? Now they'll be perfect. And the more generously cut shirt? Also great. Keep in mind that if you live in a region where seasons are a concern, the pieces you bought in the fall when you were newly pregnant may now seem a little inappropriate in spring. As best you can, make do with what you have. This initial time passes quickly, and if you need to, buy only one or two tide-me-over items. Very soon you'll regain your stamina, your energy, and yes, your figure. But for now, when you're sitting on your doughnut pillow with ice on your nether regions, you'll be happy for something—let's just say "oversized"—to wear.

Because the old saying "nine months on, nine months off" may sound absurd, but it's pretty true. "Within the first few weeks of delivery," Dr. Schiller says, "you should expect to lose fifteen pounds, including the baby, placenta, amniotic fluid, maternal fluids, and the shrinking of the uterus." After that, it generally takes about six to eight weeks for the uterus to return to its normal size. Beyond that, it's pretty much up to you. Getting back to your pre-pregnancy weight—and figure—will depend greatly on how active you are and how much weight you actually gained.

In the beginning, however, you'll be far too exhausted and sore to even think about exercise, much less losing weight, and doctors advise against trying to do any of this too early. As soon as your milk comes in and your breasts swell (and boy will they swell) you'll be amazed at the amount of food you'll need to keep the milk machine working if you choose to breastfeed. The good news about nursing is that you burn close to six hundred extra calories a day, which makes taking off the pounds a little easier. The bad news is that finding attractive nursing wear is sometimes hard. I get so many questions from clients about good-looking nursing clothes, and I tell them that I depended on comfortable, easy-access button-front shirts and snap-front tees. Both were simple and chic, and although not specifically designed for nursing, served me very well.

In the end, my advice is to be patient. You'll be a pro in no time— at nursing, changing diapers, and existing on a minimal amount of sleep. Soon you'll have the mother thing under control, and after that you'll be back to wearing your favorite clothes. In the meantime, enjoy this special time. A well-fitting pair of pants and a crisp, clean shirt may not help to soothe a crying baby, but they will make you feel pretty and put together. And that counts for a lot. The smart and sensible lessons you learned about dressing for pregnancy will serve you well in the coming weeks and beyond. Be proud that you look so good and that your fabulous sense of easy American style can carry you through everything . . . even another pregnancy!

BRAVO! YOU MADE IT.
NOW TRY TO GET SOME SLEEP . . .
I'LL SEE YOU NEXT TIME.
— LIZ